<u>Dream, Learn, Build, Grow, Stabilize</u>

The Roots of a Revolution

The Roots of a Revolution

The history of us, is the history of us all.

President: Dr. A'nyo Lee Jynnings
Vice-President: Pascal Dieujuste
Secretary: Christiana Saysay
Treasurer: Deandre Birton
SNCO Mentor: Natosha Mansker
Executive Board:
Historian: Dearon Wiley
Community Relations Advisor:
Gabriella Alband
Subcommittee Lead: Kecia Davis

The Roots of a Revolution

African American Heritage Council

*The rights of every man or woman are
diminished,
When the rights of even one man or
woman is threatened*

*There's one thing to say that you were
never taught something, and there's
another thing to not aim to educate
yourself.*

The Roots of a Revolution

Contents

Keeping the Dollar rotating 1

How to fix your credit........................17

Business Start up........................29

Use Market Research to find Customers: 46

Use competitive analysis to find a market advantage 50

Fund your business yourself with self-funding .61

Time to Bail before the crash........................79

How to File your own 89

Filing Business taxes 112

The Value of CD and Trust accounts 122

Trust account 140

Building Generational Wealth 176

Final Thought........................197

South Korea 204

Black Owned Businesses........................204

"The history of us,

Is the history of us all"

Dream, Learn, Build, Grow, Stabilize
KEEPING THE DOLLAR ROTATING

What life has taught me about being true to yourself, showing self-sufficiency, helping to build your community, and self-authenticity? Is that the pessimist sees difficulty in every opportunity. No matter the struggle or obstacle within your life, don't let yesterday take up too much of today. You need to learn more from failures than from your success because it's within failure that builds determination and focus. Without consistent work there can't be no positive change in and surrounding your verve and life.

In recent years, a movement has begun. It's a movement that takes consumers away from large, impersonal big-box retailers and introduces them back to the roots of building in their communities. People doing business with their neighbors, helping each other prosper in their very own cities. These are local farmers, craftsmen and women, antiques dealers, and other product and service providers, with items made locally and service giving locally that's sold on a small scale. When a consumer supports his/her local business owners, they enjoy benefits he/she can't possibly get from shopping at national chains. Going local does not mean gating off the outside world. It means nurturing locally owned businesses which use local resources sustainably, employ local workers at decent wages and serve primarily local consumers. It means becoming more self-sufficient and less dependent on imports. Control moves from the boardrooms of distant corporations and back into the community where it belongs.

Keeping your dollar floating within your community helps everyone within your community to win; here are some top reasons to support your local entrepreneurs, fun facts that you can't argue with:

1. It to keep our local community healthy and intact. ...
2. It supports and stimulates community relations.
3. It enables economic responsibility and wealth.
4. It builds individual and community self-sufficiency.
5. It prevents deficiency of help and resources within your community.
6. It furthers local diversity and variety.
7. It helps contribute to better Education
8. It helps create longevity jobs with a decent wage within your community.

9. It increases effectiveness and sustainability.
10. And most importantly, it helps build, secure, and stabilize help and protection for those within and surrounding your community.

The importance of buying within our community has been well documented as an avenue to strengthen not only our communities but also our culture as a whole, and most importantly followed by our economical growth; not only to provide resources, stability and jobs, but also to keep our nearly trillion-dollar buying power in our hands. Yet at times it seems impractical. But it's not impossible.

The lesson to takeaway today is if you're going to do something, do it right. If you give half the effort you will only receive half the effort. If you want a return for what you're investing in. then do it right the first time, set the bar high for yourself and the people you surround yourself with. How can the average African-American consumer do his or her part in supporting black and/or minority businesses? The answer is simple; support each other from business to customer without unbelievable high expectations. It's one thing to talk in theory about buying black; it's another thing to actually know how to do so, and supporting those that understand the value of keeping the dollar in our community. We need to educate each other on not only our value and worth but also the importance of coming together mentally, physically, emotionally, and financially to empower more of us to do it.

I want to dispel the myth that by supporting black-owned businesses you're settling for less quality in material and/or service, we need to stop having overly higher expectations of black-owned businesses than we do nonblack establishments. We need to stop being less forgiving. On the other side, as an entrepreneur and business owner you should only want to provide the best quality service and/or products to each and every customer. Remember this is not only your business at risk but also your name and reputation. For both sides the important fact to take away from this is the community should always be willing to support the businesses and the Royal Ebony and/or minority owned businesses should always be dedicated and supportive to the Royal Ebony and/or minority community. When you support each other as a whole community, Royal Ebony-owned businesses and community this and every season, you are not only investing in that specific business but also giving that business a chance to invest back into their community. The money that you spend at a Royal Ebony and/or minority-owned business is recycled back into that community. This support can make the difference between a black business succeeding or failing and that business failing can make the difference between your society prospering and flourishing or continue failing into poverty.

Nationwide, there are millions of black-owned businesses in the world. Of those businesses, only 2 out of every 10 manage to float above water and 8 out of every 10 fail on average in their first year and a half. These failures can generally be contributed to a lack of resources, stability, and growth in your community, whether it be a lack of exposure, lack of physical support and/or capital. By putting your money back into black-owned businesses and rotating that dollar back into and around your community, that money can be used for furthering the black community growth. These dollars are then recycled back into the business, as well as into black household incomes and so on. An increase in these incomes can be used toward higher education and skills and training for the black community as a whole. It's precisely this increase in support that can help people in our community reach their Goals both in education and in businesses.

Royal Ebony people spend five percent more money annually than any other race despite the fact that we are the least represented race and the race that lives in poverty at the highest rate all over the globe. This is a problem in the black community. It is a hard in your face fact that Royal Ebony people spend way more on materialistic items that holds no substance or real value but temporary admiration and once that admiration has passed we go and purchase something else that will get us feeling accepted by others temporary. We spend more on the latest electronics that we'll barely use but would cost us more than we are actually saving in our bank accounts. Some of us purchase shoes and clothes made by people that make it public they doesn't support us or people that look like us. We as a whole feed into the capitalist society that runs our world and our honor and integrity right into the ground. The fact is since black people are spending more money than every other race but holds barely even a crumb of respect from either, it would be beneficial and prosperous if more of that money were spent within the Royal Ebony communities at black owned businesses and not at the businesses that come into your community to take your money away from your community and bring it back into theirs, but supporting the actual people who actions show consistently they value the people of their community. Thus generating more wealth with the community and building a sense of commodity in helping to build back up our brothers and sisters into Monarchs. Once we realize that it is a good thing to support one another, rather than to keep feeling threatened by each other's growth and success and/or have mistrust, our communities will not only become stronger, more powerful and united but our communities will begin to get out of the survival way of living and mindset and begin to build up our own table and stop asking to be a part of or eat from another cultures table. In order for our circumstances to change, we must first change our money and our mindset, and realize the power of our dollar.

With every dollar we unfold from our purses and wallets, a story unfolds as it circulates within the economy. Understanding that story, and knowing what you can do as a business owner and as an individual consumer to keep the most of each dollar here in the home region, can make a difference to your community. Consider your dollar's influence at a store you support. The sales associates and stock clerks all collect paychecks to which your dollar contributes. The manager reorders inventory with another percentage of it. The business owner may allocate a portion towards a night out at the end of a busy week supporting another local business in the community, who then need to employ yet another unemployed person for that added customer.

The Roots of a Revolution

Small local businesses are the largest employers nationally and create two out of every three new jobs. The Small Business Act defines a small business as "one that is independently owned and operated and which is not dominant in its field of operation." Small businesses employ more than 52 percent of the nation's employees. This means that overall more Americans work for a company with fewer than 100 employees than for a large retailer, with more than 500 employees. Small businesses have played a vital role in job creation, adding more than 5 million new jobs to our economy since 2004. Buying locally means that employment levels are more likely to be stable, and may even create more opportunities for local residents to work in the community. When dollars and cents are spent locally, it just makes more sense. They can in turn be re-spent locally, raising the overall level of economic activity, paying more salaries, in turn create steady and better livelihood people inside and surrounding that area and building the local tax base. This re-circulating of money leads to an increase of economic activity, with the degree of expanse entirely dependent on the percentage of money spent locally. The Local Premium represents the quantifiable advantage to the city provided by locally owned businesses relative to chain businesses. It is the added economic benefit of local businesses to a local economy. Believe it or not, local businesses generate a substantial local premium, or added economic benefit over chain retailers. This means more money will be circulating in the local economy, which may lead to more public infrastructure like libraries and schools, and raising more money in taxable transactions to fund local government services. They're four ways in which a community can keep money local: wages and benefits paid to local residents, profits earned by local owners, the purchases of local goods and services for resale and internal use, and contributions to local nonprofits.

Here are some Examples of improvements refunding you communities can bring

1. Improve your family's health.

Buying local foods has numerous health benefits to your family. When you buy from local farmers, you have access to fruits and vegetables that you know are chemical free, as well as grass-fed meats, fresh eggs, and dairy from cows that feast on local green grass each day. There are also benefits to eating raw local honeys, which are thought to help battle different allergies.

2. Improve the local economy.

When a consumer buys local, significantly more of that money stays in the community. In fact, one study found that for every $100 spent at a local business, $68 remained in the city while only $43 of each $100 spent at a chain retailer and outside of their community. Local business owners often have incentive to support other local businesses, patronizing local establishments for both business and personal reasons. Chain businesses, on the other hand, tend to get their supplies from corporate, as well as having store managers and employees that aren't as personally invested in buying and investing back local. People that only tend to invest in themselves and not themselves and their communities, will never see the value of building for the next generation.

3. Know the people behind the product.
When you personally know the people behind the business where you're buying local products and services, you enjoy a connection you would not otherwise have. Along with the rest of the community, you celebrate when a favorite local business succeeds and you mourn when it's forced to shut its doors. This personal investment isn't quite as present when a chain business closes, aside from feeling disappointment that you have fewer businesses within convenient driving distance that will be mentally and emotional invested.

4. Keep your community unique.

Local businesses give a community its flavor and uniqueness. Towns across globe have similar chain restaurants, grocery and department stores but that diner down the street where you have breakfast at every Saturday morning is one-of-a-kind. The combined presence of your town's many local businesses makes it different from every other city in the world. By supporting those businesses instead of chains, you ensure that uniqueness is preserved as a part of your community. You ensure that the financial, emotional, and integrity structure remain in and surround your community.

5. Better customer service.

If you've ever dealt with a large corporation, you know getting help can be a nightmare. You'll call a 1-800 number, only to be transferred seven times and put on hold again. Even when you speak to a customer service representative, that person is so far removed from the decision-making process, there's little concern that the company will eventually lose you as a customer. When you shop locally, the business owner is usually directly connected to every employee in the store. That leads to a personal approach that often means any problem you have is taken seriously. Spending money with local retailers helps keep the local community alive. The places where we eat, shop, and have fun all have the potential to make a community feel like

home, having your community feeling like another Black Wall Street, Tulsa, Atlanta Georgian and Greenwood. The problem with these falling communities wasn't the fact they didn't keep the dollar rotating back into their communities, the problem was that Black Wall Street, Tulsa, Atlanta Georgian and Greenwood was easily destroyed because of the fact they were their own limitation. They didn't decide to network with each other to become a bigger entity and build a sturdy table of resources, so once people that were jealous of them decided to loot them and destroy them and their resources, they were limited to that city instead of being able to reach out to your resources to help protect each community. The term "It takes a village" is true, it takes a village to support each other and stay strong, it takes a village to education and build stability, it takes a village to help with our children and elderly, it takes a village to help each and every minority business prosper to its fullest perennial. No matter how you look at it we all need someone to lean on at time, why not it be the village?

One-of-a-kind, businesses are a fundamental part of the distinctive character and of a community. A community where large chains of shops exceed the number of independently run small businesses becomes less personal and homogenized, with less product diversity. The benefits of a thriving local independent business sector are not limited to economic benefits. Possibly equally important is that independent businesses define the community's self-image and creates a sense pride for the people who live there. National chain retailers, on the other hand, can homogenize a community and reduce its element of uniqueness and originality. Many communities are choosing to take control of their own economic character by supporting unique one-of-a-kind local businesses.

Reducing the amount of materials and products that are bought from national retail chains helps reduce your ecological footprint. Locally owned businesses can make more local purchases requiring less transportation and generally operate from within city centers as opposed to developing on the outskirts of a city. More commercial districts result in fewer vehicle miles traveled and leads to less sprawl. Less transportation also means less traffic congestion, which has the potential to reduce the amount of fuel emission that contributes to air pollution. This generally means contributing to less sprawl, congestion, wildlife, habitat loss and pollution. Locally sourced materials and products have many environmental benefits. They produce less waste by eliminating unnecessary transportation and delivery, therefore reducing the amount of packaging being used. Less packaging means less waste and less demand on landfill sites. According to the National Resource Defense Council, buying local will help reduce pollution, improve air quality and improve our health. A marketplace of hundreds of small businesses is the best way to ensure innovation and low prices over the long term. A multitude of small businesses, each selecting products based not on a national sales plan but on their own interests and the need of their local customers, guarantees a much broader range of product choices. A growing body of research shows that in an increasingly homogenized world, entrepreneurs and skilled workers are more likely to invest and settle in communities that preserve their one-of-a-kind businesses and distinctive character with multiple consumer choices.

In lean times, consumers pinch pennies and eliminate most unnecessary luxuries. From cutting back on extras to more prudent spending and budgeting, people inject a degree of caution into their financial habits. In such a volatile environment, smaller, local businesses count on your patronage in order to stay afloat; every transaction is precious to them. So when deciding where to spend your hard-earned dollars on tonight's dinner or a gift for a friend, consider the benefits of turning to local, independently owned businesses within your community. There are far-reaching advantages to deciding to "shop local." By supporting local businesses, you are in turn supporting your local economy;

Food for thought when supporting local black business:

- Local businesses are more likely to utilize other local businesses such as banks, service providers, education and farms.
- For every $100 you spend at local businesses, $50 to $68 will stay in the community.
- Independent retailers return more than three times as much money per dollar of sales back to the community in which they operate than chain competitors. Independent restaurants return more than two times as much money per dollar of sales than national restaurant chains.
- Small businesses employ 77 million people and accounted for 65% of all new jobs over the past 17 years.
- In addition to helping build the local economy, there are also notable intangible benefits that come from supporting businesses in your local community.

- Local businesses are owned and operated by your neighbors! They care about and are more invested in the well-being of your community and its future.
- Local businesses are more accountable to their local communities and donate more time, effort and money to non-profits.
- Supporting local businesses is good for the environment because they often have a smaller carbon footprint than larger companies.

In order for violence and terror to stop destroying our communities, we must as a whole get out of the survival-mode way of thinking and bring more than hope and faith in our communities. We need to bring action, wealth, unity and results. Without those four key elements, our communities will remain moving throughout life with the crab in the barrel mentality way of thinking, thinking that we're getting ahead by taking from and believing we're better than our fellow brother and sisters of this world. You could be great as an individual or choose to bask in your greatness as you and your community leaves behind a legacy.

HOW TO FIX YOUR CREDIT

Anyone and everyone can accomplish a better credit score as long as consistent effort is applied towards attaining it. Achieving a better credit score can mean qualifying for a mortgage, lower interest rate and overall better terms on a loan or credit card. If you're wondering how to fix your credit and make yourself more appealing to lenders, there are several ways to improve and repair your credit gradually over time. The best time to learn how to fix your credit score is now, the earlier you can start to build your credit history the better, a long credit history is key. So when you need approval for a loan or credit card, your score is already where it should be and standing steady. Rather than only looking for ways to raise your score, you may actually be in need of fixing something that's broken on your credit. The highest credit score is 850, but even some of the best credit scores don't reach that. Only 20% of Americans have a credit score of 800 or higher. Even if you're one of the people with the best credit score in the world, you might not still reach 850. If you know your own FICO credit score, you may wonder where you stand relative to the rest of the world consumers.

The Roots of a Revolution

The credit system is far from perfect and because of it, millions of Americans have credit scores that make them seem riskier than they are. Your credit score measures how often you pay your bills and debt on-time which is called a (payment history), or how much your credit limits called a (credit utilization ratio), and how much experience you have with managing debt called a (credit history and credit mix). Fixing your credit may be exactly what you need to do. Improving your credit score can mean qualifying for lower interest rates and better terms. That's true whether you need to purchase inventory, lease a facility, to buy and build on land, to start and/or grow your own business. The problem is, credit repair is a little like improving your professional network: You only think about it when you need it and it matters. But if you don't have good credit, it's nearly impossible to correct that situation overnight.

Fortunately, it's not too hard to improve your credit score. Review your credit reports. The credit bureaus like Trans Union, Equifax, and Experian, are required to give you a free copy of your report once a year. All you have to do is ask for your free copy. Click the links to request a copy. And apply changes. Another way to see your credit reports is to use a free service like Credit Karma. (No, I'm not endorsing Credit Karma at all but any and every avenue towards bettering yourself and your situation is a good way to grow. Me and my wife like it and think it's pretty handy, but I'm sure other free services are just as useful. Once you've signed up, you can see your credit scores and view the information contained on the reports.

Generally speaking, the entries on the different reports will be the same, but not always. For a variety of reasons credit reports are rarely identical. In the old days, you had to write letters to the credit bureaus if you wanted to dispute errors, and maybe never get back a proper response. Now a day's services like Credit Karma, Credit Saint, Creditrepaire.com etc; (again, I'm not endorsing, I'm only referencing.) let you dispute errors online. Keep in mind the score that a lender will use is likely to be different than any score you can access yourself, and the credit score itself is one of several key points of evaluation that can go into a lending decision. A credit score is a great indication of your credit health but should only be treated as a guide.

Some people will try and tell you incorrectly, that there is one true credit score when in actuality there are hundreds. FICO is the best-known credit scoring brand in America, but it has over 50 scores available. Credit score providers often tweak scoring models for different purposes. Further, each scoring model is applied in slightly different forms by the three major bureaus, making the number of available scores exponentially greater. For example, Vantage-Score is another credit scoring brand, established by the three major bureaus in 2006. Vantage-Score has three different models, each offered in slightly different forms through the three major bureaus. Each of the major credit reporting bureaus could give you a different score, even if the scoring model applied is the same. Each bureau stores its information slightly differently, with the information reported to the bureaus at different times. Each report is unique and specific to every individual spending and payment history; your credit report is a unique thumbprint that can take into account some combination of over 200 factors. If one information point varies, the final score can differ. Bottom line: Choose the credit score that you are going to track over time, and generally speaking, as that score changes, the others will, too. Pick your benchmark and stick with it.

Just make sure you get the most bang for your dispute efforts. Certain factors weigh more heavily on your credit score than others, so pay attention to those items first and for most. Secondly start with derogatory marks like collection accounts and judgments. It's not uncommon to have at least one collection account appear on your report. I had two from health care providers I used after going to the hospital; my insurance company kept claiming it had been paid while the providers said it had not, and eventually the accounts ended up with a collection agency. Eventually I decided to pay the providers and argue with the insurance company later, but both collections wound up on my credit report anyway. Fixing those problems was easy. I clicked the "Dispute" button, selected" The creditor agreed to remove my liability on this account, and within a week the dispute was resolved and the entry was removed from my credit report.

You can also dispute errors through each credit bureau. If that's your preference, go here for Trans-Union, here for Equifax, and here for Experian. Keep in mind some disputes will take longer than others. But that's fine. Once you initiate a dispute, you're done: The credit bureaus are required to investigate it and report the resolution.

Spend as much time as it takes trying to have derogatory marks removed because they also weigh heavily on your overall score. When you have a credit over nine years it helps out your average and overall credit.

Here are some helpful ways to acquire a better credit score. Be aware and hold yourself accountable and make sure that your bills don't ever turn into debt. Pay your bills on time, all of it and not just a percentage. Get credit for making utility, car, jewelry and cell phone payments on time without falling behind. Pay off debt and keep balances low on credit cards and other revolving credit. Apply for and open new credit accounts only as needed, not because it's open to you. Don't close unused credit cards, because the longer you have an account open, the better your credit will be. When managing your credit or just simply keeping our lives on track, we have to learn to work our skill-sets; the system is designed to take advantage of you, you must learn to work the system harder than it's actually working us. Because the system is designed to swallow us whole, mentally, emotionally, and physically; we all have talent, we must find out what we do individually better than anyone else and believe in that. Never let anyone tell you that it's too late to fix your credit or tell you that you're too old or too young to express your talent. Your credit is to help you stabilize your life even after you reach your dreams.

No matter what your dreams are in life, you're going to need your credit to reach it. Without credit it's nearly impossible to reach your dreams to stabilize you and your family financial goals. You can take the route of a credit repair service, but to be honest there's nothing a credit repair service can legally do for you, even removing wrong information from a credit repair service, that you can't do for yourself for little or no expense. And the cost of hiring such a company can be considerable, ranging from hundreds to thousands of dollars out of your pocket that you don't have. This is the reason why the Credit Repair organization Act was created. The Credit Repair Organizations Act is a federal law that became effective on April 1, 1997 in response to a number of consumers who had suffered from credit repair scams. In effect, the law ensures that credit repair service companies are prohibited from taking consumers' money until they fully complete the services they promise. They're required to provide consumers with a written contract stating all the services to be provided as well as the terms and conditions of payment. Under the law, consumers have three days to withdraw from the contract. They're forbidden to ask or suggest that you mislead credit reporting companies about your credit accounts or alter your identity to change your credit history. They cannot knowingly make deceptive or false claims concerning the services they are capable of offering. And they cannot ask you to sign anything that states that you are forfeiting your rights under the Credit Repair Organizations Act.

Any waiver that you sign cannot be enforced. With all of the scoring models on the market, it is unlikely that the credit score you look at will be the one your lender sees. But that's no reason not to stay up to date on your credit score and report.

How to Fix Your Credit by Yourself
There is no quick fix for your credit. Information that is negative but accurate (such as late payments and delinquencies) will remain on your credit report for 7-10 years. However, there are steps you can take to start building a more positive credit history and improve your credit scores over time. Your scores often take into account the size and recency of your debt. The bigger your debt is and the more recent your missed payments are, the worse your score will be. Bringing accounts current and continuing to pay on time will almost always have a positive impact on your credit scores. Credit scoring models usually take into account how much you owe compared to how much credit you have available, called your credit utilization rate or your balance-to-limit ratio. Basically it's the sum of all of your revolving debt (such as your credit card balances) divided by the total credit that is available to you (or the total of all your credit limits). High credit utilization rate can negatively impact your credit scores. Generally, it's a good idea to keep your credit utilization rate below 30%. For example,

if you have a $10,000 credit limit across all of your credit cards, you should try to keep your total credit card balances below $3,000 to keep your credit utilization rate low.

There are two ways to reduce your credit utilization rate:

- Reduce your debt by paying off your account balances.
- Increase your total available credit by raising your credit limit on an existing account or opening a new credit account.

While increasing your credit limit may seem like an appealing option, it can be a risky move. If increasing your credit limit tempts you to use more credit, you and your family could fall deeper into debt. Additionally, if you try to open a new credit card, an inquiry will appear on your credit report and temporarily reduce your credit score. Reducing your balances on credit cards and other revolving credit accounts is likely the better option to improve your credit utilization rate, and, subsequently, your credit scores. Consistently making on-time payments against your debt will also help you build a positive credit history, which can have additional benefits for your credit history and, by extension, your credit scores too.

The Roots of a Revolution

Your score is one of the fundamental metrics
lenders use in evaluating your application, think of
it as the first point of qualification into a lending
decision-making process. For most credit products,
you won't get approved without one score that
lenders view as acceptable. Knowing your credit
score before you apply for any new credit helps you
understand the range of interest rates you can expect
and what products you might qualify for. Twenty-
five percent of consumers identified an error on
their credit report that might affect their scores.
Your credit report is a document of how responsibly
you've managed debt in the past. All credit scoring
models look at factors like (Need I say again),
whether you pay your bills on time, how much of
your available credit you're using (it's generally
good to keep your card utilization rate under that 30
percent), the length of your credit history and how
frequently you're applying for new credit. If you
focus on managing your credit responsibly, this will
be evident on your credit report and your score will
likely take care of itself. The harder truth to
swallow is that even the best credit score might not
get you the line of credit you want. Lenders have
their own custom risk analysis models and may
require you to have a job or earn a certain amount
of money to qualify. They may balance your current
debts against your current salary to calculate your
debt burden. Some won't approve any applicant

with a bankruptcy, missed payment or account in collection on their record, no matter how their credit score has recovered.

Opening several credit accounts in a short amount of time can appear risky to lenders and negatively impact your credit score. Before you take out a loan or open a new credit card account, consider the effects it could have on your credit scores. Know too, that when you're buying a car or looking around for the best mortgage rates, your inquiries may be grouped and counted as only one inquiry for the purpose of adding information to your credit report. In many commonly-used scoring models, recent inquiries have greater effect than older inquiries, and they only appear on your credit report or a maximum of 25 months. Different models don't vary that greatly, either. No matter what score your lender ultimately looks at, each credit scoring model adheres to similar guidelines to be truly predictive, using the same base set of data from credit bureaus and similar statistical procedures. The chances of a huge fluctuation are slim. To combat these slight variances, you can shop around for credit offers to protect against the chance that one lender is looking at a credit score for you that differs a lot from the others. You can do this without impacting your credit score, too. If you're applying for a mortgage or auto loan, Vantage-

Score treats all inquiries made within a two-week window as one hard pull, while FICO lumps all similar inquiries within 30 days together. However, while you may not be able to change information from the past, you can demonstrate good credit management moving forward by paying your bills on time and as agreed. As you build a positive credit history, over time, your credit scores will likely improve.

BUSINESS START UP

One of the hardest easiest things to do in the world is to live in this world chasing the dream of someone's else opinion; but in reality it is easy in solitude to live after our own; a great man/woman is who in the midst of the crowd keeps with perfect sweetness the independence and structure of solitude. Talk to any entrepreneur or small business owner and you'll quickly learn that starting a business requires a lot of work, and unique individualism, a business as a whole, even though building any business is a team effort. An idea doesn't become a business without effort. Hello my name is Dr. A'nyo Jynnings; I am the president of the African American Heritage Council (AAHC.) My hard working council and I aim to bring growth, understanding and content with substance in your life. Information should flow through us all freely and transparently, that's the only way life can be fruitful and truly prosperous for all. Starting a business can either feel like a breath of fresh air or a tighten noose. the difference is simple, rushing over carefully planning. Rushing is having the mindset to try to chase every dollar before even having your business goals, focus, and structure complete. Carefully playing, is focusing on your product or service for sale, and setting goals to gain the attention of your targeting audience, never spending over 40% of the total of what your business. You want to make sure you prepare thoroughly before starting a business, but realize that things will almost certainly go awry. To run a successful business, you must adapt to changing situations. Before you start selling your product or service, you need to build up your brand and get a following of people who are ready to jump when you open your doors for business. Conducting in-depth market research on your field and the demographics of your potential clientele is an important part of crafting a business plan. This involves running surveys, holding focus groups, and researching SEO and public data. Some budding entrepreneurs understand the effort necessary to create a business, but they might not be familiar with the many steps required to launch a business venture. If you're willing to put in the effort to build a business, you're going to want to know the steps needed to reach your goals.

Another option is to open up a franchise of an established company. The concept, brand following and business model are already in place; all you need is a good location and the means to fund your operation.

Business plans help you run your business

A good business plan guides you through each stage of starting and managing your business. You'll use your business plan as a roadmap for how to structure, run, and grow your new business. It's a way to think through the key elements of your business. Business plans can help you get funding or bring on new business partners. Investors want to feel confident they'll see a return on their investment. Your business plan is the tool you'll use to convince people that working with you, or investing in your company, is a smart choice.

Pick a business plan format that works for you

There's no right or wrong way to write up a business plan. What's important is that your plan meets your needs. Most business plans fall into one of two common categories: traditional or lean startup. Traditional business plans are more common, use a standard structure, and encourage you to go into detail in each section. They tend to require more work upfront and can be dozens of pages long. Lean startup business plans are less common but still use a standard structure. They focus on summarizing only the most important points of the key elements of your plan. They can take as little as one hour to make and are typically only one page.

Tasks like naming the business and creating a logo are obvious, but what about the less-heralded, equally important steps? Whether it's determining your business structure or crafting a detailed marketing strategy, the workload can quickly pile up. Rather than spinning your wheels and guessing at where to start, follow this 14-steps checklist to transform your business from a light-bulb above your head to a real entity.

1. Refine your idea
2. Write up a realistic business plan
3. Assess your finances
4. keep to your budget
5. Determine your legal business structure
6. Check if your business name is available
7. Register with the government and IRS
8. Purchase an insurance policy
9. Build your business structure
10. Build your team
11. Choose your vendors
12. Brand yourself and advertise
13. Grow your business and never become complacent

14. Always remember, spending half or more money than you're bringing in is working backwards

If you're thinking about starting a business, you likely already have an idea of what you want to sell, or at least the market you want to enter. Do a quick search for existing companies in your chosen industry. Learn what current brand leaders are doing and figure out how you can do it better. If you think your business can deliver something other companies don't (or deliver the same thing, only faster and cheaper), you've got a solid idea and are ready to create a business plan. It is always good to know why you are launching your business. In this process, it may be wise to differentiate between whether; the business serves a personal why or a marketplace why. When your why is focused on meeting a need in the marketplace, the scope of your business will always be larger than a business that is designed to serve a personal need.

Traditional Business Plan
This type of plan is very detailed, takes more time to write, and is comprehensive. Lenders and investors commonly request this plan.

Lean Startup plan

This type of plan is high-level focus, fast to write, and contains key elements only. Some lenders and investors may ask for more information.

Traditional business plan format

You might prefer a traditional business plan format if you're very detail oriented, want a comprehensive plan, or plan to request financing from traditional sources. When you write your business plan, you don't have to stick to the exact business plan outline. Instead, use the sections that make the most sense for your business and your needs. Traditional business plans use some combination of these nine sections.

Executive summary

Briefly tell your reader what your company is and why it will be successful. Include your mission statement, your product or service, and basic information about your company's leadership team, employees, and location. You should also include financial information and high-level growth plans if you plan to ask for financing.

Company description

Use your company description to provide detailed information about your company. Go into detail about the problems your business solves. Be specific, and list out the consumers, organization, or businesses your company plans to serve. Explain the competitive advantages that will make your business a success. Are there experts on your team? Have you found the perfect location for your store? Your company description is the place to boast about your strengths.

Market analysis

You'll need a good understanding of your industry outlook and target market. Competitive research will show you what other businesses are doing and what their strengths are. In your market research, look for trends and themes. What do successful competitors do? Why does it work? Can you do it better? Now is the best time to answer these questions.

Marketing and sales

There's no single way to approach a marketing strategy. Your strategy should evolve and change to fit your unique needs. Your goal in this section is to describe how you'll attract and retain customers. You'll also describe how a sale will actually happen. You'll refer to this section later when you make financial projections, so make sure to thoroughly describe your complete marketing and sales strategies.

Funding request

If you're asking for funding, this is where you'll outline your funding requirements. Your goal is to clearly explain how much funding you'll need over the next five years and what you'll use it for. Specify whether you want debt or equity, the terms you'd like applied, and the length of time your request will cover. Give a detailed description of how you'll use your funds. Specify if you need funds to buy equipment or materials, pay salaries, or cover specific bills until revenue increases. Always include a description of your future strategic financial plans, like paying off debt or selling your business.

Financial projections

Supplement your funding request with financial projections. Your goal is to convince the reader that your business is stable and will be a financial success. If your business is already established, include income statements, balance sheets, and cash flow statements for the last three to five years. If you have other collateral you could put against a loan, make sure to list it now.

Provide a prospective financial outlook for the next five years. Include forecasted income statements, balance sheets, cash flow statements, and capital expenditure budgets. For the first year, be even more specific and use quarterly, or even monthly, projections. Make sure to clearly explain your projections, and match them to your funding requests. This is a great place to use graphs and charts to tell the financial story of your business.

Appendix

Use your appendix to provide supporting documents or other materials were specially requested. Common items to include are credit histories, resumes, product pictures, letters of reference, licenses, permits, or patents, legal documents, permits, and other contracts.

Organization and management

Tell your reader the importance of your product and how your company will be structured and who will run it.

Describe the legal structure of your business. State whether you have or intend to incorporate your business as a C or an S corporation, form a general or limited partnership, or if you're a sole proprietor or LLC. Use an organizational chart to lay out who's in charge of what in your company. Show how each person's unique experience will contribute to the success of your venture. Consider including resumes and CVs of key members of your team.

Service or product line

Describe what you sell or what service you offer. Explain how it benefits your customers and what the product lifecycle looks like. Share your plans for intellectual property, like copyright or patent filings. If you're doing research and development for your service or product, explain it in detail.

Forming a Limited Liability Corporation (LLC)

A Limited Liability Corporation ("LLC") holds the owners, or members, to limited liability. One benefit of an LLC includes member's personal assets being protected if the business is sued. The documents needed for starting an LLC include:

- Name of the LLC
- Articles of Organization
- Business Name & Location
- Business Purpose & Structure
- Registered Agent
- LLC Operating Agreement
- Percentage of Ownership Per Member
- Percentage of Profits/Gains Each Member Receives
- Each Members Voting Rights
- Dissolving of LLC/Membership
- Selling or Gifting of Member Interest
- Necessary licenses and Permits (depending on business)

The Roots of a Revolution

For most new business owners, the best option is to form your LLC in the state where you live and where you plan to conduct your business. If your business will have a physical presence (storefronts, offices, sales reps, etc.) in different states, then you will need to register a foreign LLC in every state where you will do business. There are sometimes benefits to forming your LLC in a state that has business-friendly laws, such as Delaware or Nevada. However, this is rarely worth the extra fees and paperwork of having to register your LLC in multiple states.

Choosing your business name is the first step in forming an LLC. Every state has its own rules about what kinds of names are allowed for LLCs. In general, you will need to observe these guidelines:

- Your name ***must include*** the phrase "limited liability company," or one of its abbreviations (LLC or L.L.C.).
- Your name ***cannot include*** words that could confuse your LLC with a government agency (FBI, Treasury, State Department, etc.).
- Restricted words (e.g. Bank, Attorney, and University) ***may require*** additional paperwork and a licensed individual, such as a doctor or lawyer, to be part of your LLC.

A registered agent is a person or business that sends and receives legal papers on your behalf.
These documents include official correspondence like legal summons and document filings, which your registered agent will receive and forward to you. Most states require every LLC to nominate a registered agent. Your registered agent must be a resident of the state you're doing business in, or a corporation authorized to conduct business in that state. A registered agent is an individual or business entity that accepts tax and legal documents on behalf of your business. A registered agent is also known as a resident agent or statutory agent. Most states require you to have an LLC registered agent. The agent can be a professional service, yourself, or a colleague given they meet the state's criteria.

Next prepare an operating agreement describes how you will run your LLC. It contains important information about the way your business will be managed, the contributions of the LLC members and the way profits and losses will be divided. Your operating agreement will also explain the procedures for admitting new members and dealing with departing members. If these matters are not addressed in the operating agreement, some states require you to dissolve the LLC if a member leaves. The operating agreement isn't filed with the state. You should keep it in a file or binder with your other important business records. Now that you've laid the groundwork, you're ready to prepare articles of organization. This is the document that you'll file with the state to establish your LLC. A form for the articles is available on the website of your state business filing agency. Each state has its own requirements for the articles of organization, but in general you will need to include:

- The name of your LLC.
- The duration of your LLC, if it is not perpetual.
- The purpose for which your LLC was formed. In most states, you can state a broad, general purpose.
- The name and address of the registered agent.
- Whether the LLC will be managed by its members or by managers.

The person forming the LLC must sign the articles, and in some states the registered agent must also sign. You must submit the articles and a filing fee to your state's business filing agency. You may be able to file the articles online, or you may need to submit them in person or by mail.

The Roots of a Revolution

Processing times may vary from a few days to a few weeks, depending on your state. Some states offer expedited processing for an additional fee. You will receive a certificate when the LLC has been officially formed.

A few states have an additional requirement: you must publish a small newspaper notice of your intent to form an LLC. This notice usually must be published several times over a period of weeks, and you must then submit an affidavit to the state business filing agency. There may be fees associated with this notice that have to be paid to the newspaper or to the state government. Check with your Secretary of State for the requirements in your state.

Now that your LLC is official, you can obtain a federal tax ID number and set up a business bank account. Depending on your business, you may also need to register your LLC with state and local taxing, licensing and permitting authorities. And if you are doing business in more than one state, you will need to register to do business in those additional states. Setting up an LLC isn't difficult, but it's important to follow your state's requirements. And once your LLC is established, you'll have gained important protection for yourself and your business.

The Roots of a Revolution

Forming a Corporation

Similar to an LLC, in a Corporation the owners, or shareholders, are also limited in their liability. Ownership can easily be transferred through a sale or gift of shares. In order to start a Corporation you must file:

- Reservation of Corporate Name
- Articles of Incorporation
- Corporate Bylaws
- Rights/Responsibilities of Shareholders
- Corporation Purpose & Structure
- Stock Certificates
- Necessary licenses and Permits (depending on business)

New business owners have numerous goals when they're starting out, including rapid growth and recognition for their fledgling venture. But overnight success isn't often the standard: There's no specific "special sauce" to add to the recipe for instant results, and nothing is guaranteed. However, there are ways to reach growth milestones that can catapult a business to success.

But before you can even think about your company's growth trajectory, you need to ensure that you have a solid staff that can help you achieve it. With a small business looking to grow, it's important to have the right players at the table, they need to be people who aren't afraid to roll up their sleeves. The words 'That's not my job,' do not exist in their vocabulary. They have to be dedicated to the mission of their own success in order to be dedicated to the mission of your company's success. Hiring the absolute best people you can is a surefire way to ensure fast growth, it's all about having the right team.

Focus on established revenue sources, rather than trying to acquire new customers, direct your attention to the core customers you already have, you can do this by implementing a referral or customer loyalty program, or trying out marketing strategies based on previous purchase behaviors to encourage repeat business. This focus on your established market is especially important if you're trying to get funding. In the past, we would highlight our business goal to become a franchise, which didn't resonate with banks, we learned to emphasize that there is a large market for what we do. This would pique a banker's interest because he or she cares about the return and risk on investments more than your business aspirations. Risk is an inevitable part of starting and growing a business. It's impossible to control everything, but there are plenty of ways to limit internal and external threats to your company and its growth.

One important resource to help you accomplish this is your business insurance provider.

USE MARKET RESEARCH TO FIND CUSTOMERS:

Market research blends consumer behavior and economic trends to confirm and improve your business idea. Market research can be used in identifying customer needs, as well as who they are. You have to ask the right questions though. If you don't really know your customers you will not retain them leaving you constantly chasing after new ones. Don't just follow your instincts as many companies do. It's crucial to understand your consumer base from the outset. Market research lets you reduce risks even while your business is still just a gleam in your eye. Gather demographic information to better understand opportunities and limitations for gaining customers. This could include population data on age, wealth, family, interests, or anything else that's relevant for your business.

Then answer these questions to get a good sense of your market ability.

- **Demand:** Is there a desire for your product or service?
- **Market size:** How many people would be interested in your offering?

- **Economic indicators:** What is the income range and employment rate?
- **Location:** Where do your customers live and where can your business reach?
- **Market saturation:** How many similar options are already available to consumers?
- **Pricing:** What do potential customers pay for these alternatives?

Market researchers are motivated by two things, praise or reward. It's kind of funny, whether you are 3 years old or 53 years old, it's the same thing just two sides of the same coin. I can make my son do chores or homework without a fight simply by offering him snakes. I know I am willing to go the extra mile for an adult version of snakes, who am I kidding? Adult size real ice cream still works for me too. The point is how do you motivate and keep your customers Interested?

Achieving this is not just as simple as asking the right questions. There are many details to figure out and it is highly recommended that you use experienced researchers or consultants:

For example:

- How do you define which customers to talk to?

- How do you decide on a format for your research?
- How do you know what type of questions to ask to get to know your customers?
- What attributes or demographics are important in getting to know your customers?
- How do you use the data once it is collected?

Surveys are the staple of market research, however you have to know how and when to use the three types of questions: Opened-Ended, Closed-Ended and Strategic. Opened-ended questions can provide a lot of information, but often they do not provide all the detail you need. The short answers you get from Closed-Ended questions can often grind a conversation to a halt. Strategic questions tend to treat the customer as the expert and lead to a deeper conversation which in turn helps you really know how you can help that customer. Giving the customer more freedom in answering your question lets them provide you with their agenda (not yours).

You'll also want to keep up with the latest small business trends. It's important to gain a sense of the specific market share that will impact your profits.

The Roots of a Revolution

You can do market research using existing sources, or you can do the research yourself and go direct to consumers.

Existing sources can save you a lot of time and energy, but the information might not be as specific to your audience as you'd like. Use it to answer questions that are both general and quantifiable, like industry trends, demographics, and household incomes. Asking consumers yourself can give you a nuanced understanding of your specific target audience. But, direct research can be time consuming and expensive. Use it to answer questions about your specific business or customers, like reactions to your logo, improvements you could make to buying experience, and where customers might go instead of your business.

Here are a few methods you can use to do direct research:

- Surveys
- Questionnaires
- Focus groups
- In-depth interviews

For guidance on deciding which methods are worthwhile for your small business, the Small Business Administration provides counseling services through our restructure Network.

USE COMPETITIVE ANALYSIS TO FIND A MARKET ADVANTAGE

Competitive analysis helps you learn from businesses competing for your potential customers. This is key to defining a competitive edge that creates sustainable revenue. Your competitive analysis should identify your competition by product line or service and market segment. Assess the following characteristics of the competitive landscape:

- Market share
- Prioritize
- Realize the difference between what your business needs and what your business wants.
- Strengths and weaknesses
- Your window of opportunity to enter the market
- The importance of your target market to your competitors
- Any barriers that may hinder you as you enter the market
- Indirect or secondary competitors who may impact your success

The Roots of a Revolution

Several industries might be competing to serve the same market you're targeting. That's why you should make sure to differentiate your competitive analysis by industry. There are many methods for doing this. Important industry factors to consider include level of competition, threat of new competitors or services, and the effect of suppliers and customers on price. Meet clients (and competitors) and strategize your next move, instead of just moving.

It costs money to start a business. Funding your business is one of the first, and most important, financial choices most business owners make. How you choose to fund your business could affect how you structure and run your business.

Your launch and first sales are only the beginning of your task as an entrepreneur. To make a profit and stay afloat, you always need to be growing your business. It's going to take time and effort, but you'll get out of your business what you put into it. Collaborating with more established brands in your industry is a great way to achieve growth. Reach out to other companies, privet organizations etc and ask for some promotion in exchange for a free product sample or service. Partner with a few charity organizations, and volunteer some of your time or products to get your name out there.

The Roots of a Revolution

While searching for tips online can and will help launch your business and get you set to grow, there's never a perfect plan. You want to make sure you prepare thoroughly for starting a business, but things will almost certainly go awry. To run a successful business, you must adapt to changing situations. Be prepared to adjust, There's a saying in the military that no plan survives the first contact, meaning that you can have the best plan in the world, but as soon as it's in action, things can change, and you have to be ready and willing to adapt and problem-solve quickly. As an entrepreneur, your value lies in solving problems whether that is your product or service solving problems for other people or you solving problems within your organization.

Small businesses need to manage their growth to avert disruptions that can bring business to a grinding halt; For example, the theft of employee data, customer records and product designs can destroy a small business, generating significant costs and eroding customer confidence and loyalty. Not every business owner's policy covers data breaches or other cyber losses. Small businesses should be prepared by seeking insurance products that help them recover, including those that cover the cost of remediation and lawsuits. As small businesses grow, they may add space or equipment, create new products or services, or increase their operating and distribution footprint, so the AAHC advise you to periodically reviewing your policy to ensure you have the right coverage. It's easy to forget this step amid rapid expansion, but you don't want to find out that you've outgrown your coverage just when you need it the most, one trait that successful startups often have in common is the ability to switch directions quickly in response to changes in the market. An agile approach to development, both in terms of your product and your company, will help you grow more quickly. By allowing yourself to adapt and change quickly, you're able to test different approaches to business and find out what works best, It allows you to fail, pick yourself back up and keep going.

There are many reliable sources that provide customer and market information at no cost. Free statistics are readily available to help prospective small business owners. If you're feeling uninspired, the first thing you need to look at is whether your business actually has a future or not. How are your competitors doing? Do they seem to be having similar difficulties and challenges, or are they steaming ahead of you? This is a great way to check whether all businesses within your sector are struggling, or (no offence) whether it's just you.

The Roots of a Revolution

Before trying to jump out there and pushing your brand, try branding yourself first. Before you start selling your product or service, you need to build up your brand and get a following of people ready to jump when you open your literal or figurative doors for business. Create a logo that can help people easily identify your brand, and be consistent in using it across all of your platforms, including your all-important company website. Use the power of social media in your favor to spread the word about your new business, perhaps as a promotional tool to offer coupons and discounts to followers once you launch. Be sure to also keep these digital assets up to date with relevant, interesting content about yourself, your business, your product/service and industry.

Too many startups have the wrong mindset about their websites. The issue is they see their website as a cost, not an investment, in today's digital age that's a huge mistake. The small business owners who understand how critical it is to have a great online presence will have a leg up on starting out strong. Creating a marketing plan that goes beyond just your launch and monthly promotions, a structured market plan is essential to building a clientele by continually getting the word out about your business. This process, especially in the beginning, is just as important as providing a quality product or service. Ask customers to opt-in to your marketing communications as you build your brand, ask your customers and potential customers for permission to communicate with them. The easiest way to do this is by using opt-in forms. These are "forms of consent" given by web users, authorizing you to contact them with further information about your business. These types of forms usually pertain to email communication and are often used in e-commerce to request permission to send newsletters, marketing material, product sales, etc. to customers. Folks get so many throwaway emails and other messages these days, that by getting them to opt-in to your services in a transparent way, you begin to build trust with your customers. Customers' perceptions of your business can really make or break a business. Deliver quality experiences and products, and they'll quickly sing your praises on social media; mess it up, and they'll tell the world even faster. Fast growth depends on making your current and potential customers happy with their experience.

The Opt-in forms are a great starting point for building trust and respect with potential customers. However, it's important to know that these forms are required by law. The CAN-SPAM Act of 2003 sets requirements for commercial email by the Federal Trade Commission. This law doesn't just apply to bulk email; it covers all commercial messages in which the law defines as "any electronic mail message the primary purpose of which is the commercial advertisement or promotion of a commercial product or service." Each email in violation of this law is subject to fines of more than $40,000. Despite its name, the CAN-SPAM Act doesn't apply just to bulk email. It covers all commercial messages, which the law defines as including email that promotes content on commercial websites. The law makes no exception for business-to-business email. That means all emails, take for example, a message to former customers announcing a new product line, must comply with the law.

Each separate email in violation of the CAN-SPAM Act is subject to penalties of up to $43,280, so non-compliance can be costly. But following the law isn't complicated. Here's a rundown of CAN-SPAM's main requirements:

- **Don't use false or misleading header information.** Your "From," "To," "Reply-To," and routing information, including the originating domain name and email address, must be accurate and identify the person or business who initiated the message.

- **Don't use deceptive subject lines.** The subject line must accurately reflect the content of the message.
- **Identify the message as an ad.** The law gives you a lot of leeway in how to do this, but you must disclose clearly and conspicuously that your message is an advertisement.
- **Tell recipients where you're located.** Your message must include your valid physical postal address. This can be your current street address, a post office box you've registered with the U.S. Postal Service, or a private mailbox you've registered with a commercial mail receiving agency established under Postal Service regulations.
- **Tell recipients how to opt out of receiving future email from you.** Your message must include a clear and conspicuous explanation of how the recipient can opt out of getting email from you in the future. Craft the notice in a way that's easy for an ordinary person to recognize, read, and understand. Creative use of type size, color, and location can improve clarity. Give a return email address or another easy Internet-based way to allow people to communicate their choice to you. You may create a menu to allow a recipient to opt out of certain types of

messages, but you must include the option to stop all commercial messages from you. Make sure your spam filter doesn't block these opt-out requests.

- **Honor opt-out requests promptly.** Any opt-out mechanism you offer must be able to process opt-out requests for at least 30 days after you send your message. You must honor a recipient's opt-out request within 10 business days. You can't charge a fee, require the recipient to give you any personally identifying information beyond an email address, or make the recipient take any step other than sending a reply email or visiting a single page on an Internet website as a condition for honoring an opt-out request. Once people have told you they don't want to receive more messages from you, you can't sell or transfer their email addresses, even in the form of a mailing list. The only exception is that you may transfer the addresses to a company you've hired to help you comply with the CAN-SPAM Act.

- **Monitor what others are doing on your behalf.** The law makes clear that even if you hire another company to handle your email marketing, you can't contract away your legal responsibility to comply with the law. Both the company whose product is promoted in the message and the company that actually sends the message may be held legally responsible.

Consider these types of business statistics in your market research and competitive analysis:

The Focus:
The Realistic Goal:
General business statistics
   Find statistics on industries, business conditions
Consumer statistics
Gain info on potential customers, consumer markets
Demographics
Segment the population for targeting customers
Economic indicators
Know unemployment rates, loans granted and more
Employment statistics
Dig deeper into employment trends for your market
Income statistics
Pay your employees fair rates based on earnings data
Money and interest rates
Keep money by mastering exchange and interest rates
Production and sales statistics
Understand demand, costs and consumer spending
Trade statistics
Track indicators of sales and market performance

The Roots of a Revolution

Statistics of specific industries
Use a wealth of federal agency data on industries

FUND YOUR BUSINESS YOURSELF WITH SELF-FUNDING

Otherwise known as bootstrapping, self-funding lets you leverage your own financial resources to support your business. Self-funding can come in the form of turning to family and friends for capital, using your savings accounts, or even tapping into your 401k. With self-funding, you retain complete control over the business but you also take on all the risk yourself. Be careful not to spend more than you can afford, and be especially careful if you choose to use tap into retirement accounts early. You might face expensive fees or penalties, or damage your ability to retire on time, so you should check with your plan's administrator and a personal financial advisor first.

Next step is finding quality investors.
Investors can give you funding to start your business in the form of venture capital investments. Venture capital is normally offered in exchange for an ownership share and active role in the company. Venture capital differs from traditional financing in a number of important ways. Venture capital typically:

- Focuses high-growth companies

The Roots of a Revolution

- Invests capital in return for equity, rather than debt (it's not a loan)
- Takes higher risks in exchange for potential higher returns
- Has a longer investment horizon than traditional financing

Almost all venture capitalists will, at a minimum, want a seat on the board of directors. So be prepared to give up some portion of both control and ownership of your company in exchange for funding.

Determine how much funding you'll need

Every business has different needs, and no financial solution is one size fits all. Your personal financial situation and vision for your business will shape the financial future of your business. Once you know how much startup funding you'll need, it's time to figure out how you'll get it.

How to get venture capital funding

There's no guaranteed way to get venture capital, but the process generally follows a standard order of basic steps.

1. ***Find an investor***
   Look for individual investors, sometimes called "angel investors", or venture capital

firms. Be sure to do enough background research to know if the investor is reputable and has experience working with startup companies.

2. ***Share your business plan***
   The investor will review your business plan to make sure it meets their investing criteria. Most investment funds concentrate on an industry, geographic area, or stage of business development.

3. ***Go through due diligence review***
   The investors will look at your company's management team, market, products and services, corporate governance documents, and financial statements.

4. ***Work out the terms***
   If they want to invest, the next step is to agree on a term sheet that describes the terms and conditions for the fund to make an investment.

5. ***Investment***
   Once you agree on a term sheet, you can get the investment! Once a venture fund has invested, it becomes actively involved in the company. Venture funds normally come in

"rounds." As the company meets milestones, further rounds of financing are made available, with adjustments in price as the company executes its plan.

Use crowd-funding to fund your business

Crowd-funding raises funds for a business from a large number of people, called crowd-funders. Crowd-funders aren't technically investors, because they don't receive a share of ownership in the business and don't expect a financial return on their money.

Instead, crowd-funders expect to get a "gift" from your company as thanks for their contribution. Often, that gift is the product you plan to sell or other special perks, like meeting the business owner or getting their name in the credits. This makes crowd-funding a popular option for people who want to produce creative works (like a documentary), or a physical product (like a high-tech cooler).

Crowd-funding is also popular because it's very low risk for business owners. Not only do you get to retain full control of your company, but if your plan fails, you're typically under no obligation to repay your crowd-funders. Every crowd-funding platform is different, so make sure to read the fine print and understand your full financial and legal obligations.

Get a small business loan

If you want to retain complete control of your business, but don't have enough funds to start, consider a small business loan. To increase your chances of securing a loan, you should have a business plan, expense sheet, and financial projections for the next five years. These tools will give you an idea of how much you'll need to ask for, and will help the bank know they're making a smart choice by giving you a loan. Once you have your materials ready, contact banks and credit unions to request a loan. You'll want to compare offers to get the best possible terms for your loan.

Use Lender Match to find lenders who offer SBA-guaranteed loans

If you have trouble getting a traditional business loan, you should look into SBA-guaranteed loans. When a bank thinks your business is too risky to lend money to, the SBA can agree to guarantee your loan. That way, the bank has less risk and is more willing to give your business a loan. Use "Lender Match" to find lenders who offer SBA-guaranteed loans. They're also, (Small Business Administration investment) programs out there as well. A small business investment Company (SBIC), SBIC's are privately owned and managed investment funds licensed and regulated by the Small Business Administration. They use their own capital, plus funds borrowed with an SBA guarantee, to make equity and debt investments in qualifying small businesses. There's no better time like the present, it's time to balance it with a little reality. Does your idea have the potential to succeed?

You will need to run your business idea through a validation process before you go any further. In order for a small business to be successful, it must solve a problem, fulfill a need or offer something the market wants.

- Is there a need for your anticipated products/services?
- Who needs it?
- Are there other companies offering similar products/services now?
- What is the competition like?
- How will your business fit into the market?

A business plan blueprint is a blueprint that will guide your business from the start-up phase through establishment and eventually business growth, and it is a must-have for all new businesses. The good news is that there are different types of business plans for different types of businesses. If you intend to seek financial support from an investor or financial institution, before SBA-loans and bank loans, finding quality people with integrity and substance of heart and mind as investor is a good way to go when doing a traditional business plan is a must.

This type of business plan is generally long and thorough and has a common set of sections that investors and banks look for when they are validating your idea. If you don't anticipate seeking financial support, a simple one-page business plan can give you clarity about what you hope to achieve and how you plan to do it. In fact, you can even create a working business plan on the back of a napkin, and improve it over time. Some kind of plan in writing is always better than nothing.

No matter what you may think, starting a small business doesn't have to require a lot of money, but it will involve some initial investment as well as the ability to cover ongoing expenses before you are turning a profit. Put together a spreadsheet that estimates the one-time startup costs for your business (licenses and permits, equipment, legal fees, insurance, branding, market research, inventory, trade marking, grand opening events, property leases, etc.), as well as what you anticipate you will need to keep your business running for at least 12 months (rent, utilities, marketing and advertising, production, supplies, travel expenses, employee salaries, your own salary, etc.).

Those numbers combined is the initial investment you will need. You can also attempt to get your business off the ground by bootstrapping, using as little capital as necessary to start your business. You may find that a combination of the paths listed above work best. The goal here, though, is to work through the options and create a plan for setting up the capital you need to get your business off the ground.

You see the African American Heritage Counsel (AAHC) is all about mental, physical, and emotional self-sufficiency and structure, and so should your business be about self-sufficiency and structure. Your small business can be a sole proprietorship, a partnership, a limited liability company (LLC) or a corporation. The business entity you choose will impact many factors from your business name, to your liability, to how you file your taxes. You may choose an initial business structure, and then reevaluate and change your structure as your business grows and needs change.

Depending on the complexity of your business, it may be worth investing in a consultation from an attorney or CPA to ensure you are making the right structure choice for your business. Your business name plays a role in almost every aspect of your business, so you want it to be a good one. Make sure you think through all of the potential implications as you explore your options and choose your business name, a business name that fits your brand and not your ego.

Once you have chosen a name for your business, you will need to check if it's trademarked or currently in use. Then, you will need to register it. A sole proprietor must register their business name with either their state or county clerk. Corporations, LLCs, or limited partnerships typically register their business name when the formation paperwork is filed. Paperwork is a part of the process when you start your own business.

There are a variety of small business licenses and permits that may apply to your situation, depending on the type of business you are starting and where you are located. You will need to research what licenses and permits apply to your business during the start-up process. Starting any business has a price, so you need to determine how you're going to cover those costs. Do you have the means to fund your startup, or will you need to borrow money? If you're planning to leave your current job to focus on your business, do you have money put away to support yourself until you make a profit? It's best to find out how much your start-up costs will be. Many startups fail because they run out of money before turning a profit. It's never a bad idea to overestimate the amount of startup capital you need, as it can be a while before the business begins to bring in sustainable revenue.

Perform a break-even analysis.
One way you can determine how much money you need is to perform a break-even analysis this is an essential element of financial planning that helps business owners determine when their company, product or service will be profitable.

You can always try this simple formula to familiarize yourself with a break-even analysis:

Fixed Costs / (Average Price – Variable Costs)
Break-Even Point

Every entrepreneur should use this formula as a tool because it informs you about the minimum performance your business must achieve to avoid losing money. Furthermore, it helps you understand exactly where your profits come from, so you can set production goals accordingly. Here are the three most common reasons to conduct a break-even analysis:

Determine profitability. This is generally every business owner's highest interest. Ask yourself: How much revenue do I need to generate to cover all my expenses? Which products or services turn a profit and which ones are sold at a loss?

Price a product or service. When most people think about pricing, they consider how much their product costs to create and how competitors are pricing their products. Ask yourself: What are the fixed rates, what are the variable costs, and what is the total cost? What is the cost of any physical goods and what is the cost of labor?

Analyze the data. What volumes of goods or services do you have to sell to be profitable? Ask yourself: How can I reduce my overall fixed costs? How can I reduce the variable costs per unit? How can I improve sales?

Watch your expenses.
Courage is the most important of all the virtues because without courage, you can't practice any other virtue consistently, but stupidity is just simply stupidity. There's a fine line in being courageous and just being reckless, realize when you're trying to keep up with the joneses for no reason. Don't overspend when starting a business. Understand the types of purchases that make sense for your

business and avoid overspending on fancy new equipment that won't help you reach your business goals. A lot of startups tend to spend money on unnecessary things, take for example: If we worked with a startup that had two employees but spent a huge amount on office space that would fit 20 people. They also leased a professional high-end printer that was more suited for a team of 100 (it had keycards to track who was printing what and when). Spend as little as possible when you start and only on the things that are essential for the business to grow and be a success. Luxuries can come when you're established and have a firmly built structure.

Businesses especially startups, requiring significant funding upfront may want to bring on an quality investor. Investors can provide several million dollars or more to a fledgling company, with the expectation that the backers will have a hands-on role in running your business. Alternatively, I say again, you could launch an equity crowfunding campaign to raise smaller amounts of money from multiple backers. Crowfunding has helped numerous companies in recent years, and there are dozens of reliable crowdfunding platforms designed for different types of businesses.

Choose the right business bank.

Open a business account when you're ready to start accepting or spending money as your business. A business bank account helps you stay legally compliant and protected. It also provides benefits to your customers and employees. As soon as you start accepting or spending money as your business, you should open a business bank account. Common business accounts include a checking account, savings account, credit card account, and a merchant services account. Merchant services accounts allow you to accept credit and debit card transactions from your customers. A small business checking account can help you handle legal, tax, and day-to-day issues. The good news is it's easy to set one up if you have the right registrations and paperwork ready. When choosing the right business bank, size matters.

Some things to keep an eye out for when in search for a great business bank:

- **Protection.** Business banking offers limited personal liability protection by keeping your business funds separate from your personal funds. Merchant services also offer purchase protection for your customers and ensures that their personal information is secure.

- **Professionalism.** Customers will be able to pay you with credit cards and make checks out to your business instead of directly to you. Plus, you'll be able to authorize employees to handle day-to-day banking tasks on behalf of the business.
- **Preparedness.** Business banking usually comes with the option for a line of credit for the company. This can be used in the event of an emergency, or if your business needs new equipment.
- **Purchasing power.** Credit card accounts can help your business make large startup purchases and help establish a credit history for your business.

AAHC, recommends finding smaller community banks because they are in tune with the local market conditions and will work with you based on your overall business profile and character. They're unlike big banks that look at your credit score and will be more selective to loan money to small businesses, Not only that, but small banks want to build a personal relationship with you and ultimately help you if you run into problems and miss a payment.

Some business owners open a business account at the same bank they use for their personal accounts.

The Roots of a Revolution

Rates, fees, and options vary from bank to bank, so you should shop around to make sure you find the lowest fees and the best benefits like here are some things to consider when you're looking to open up a business checking or savings account:

1. Introductory offers
2. Interest rates for savings and checking
3. Interest rates for lines of credit
4. Transaction fees
5. Early termination fees
6. Minimum account balance fees

Or if you're interested in opening up a merchant services account:

1. **Discount rate:** The percentage charged for every transaction processed.
2. **Transaction fees:** The amount charged for every credit card transaction.
3. **ACH daily batch fees:** Fees charged when you settle credit card transactions for that day.
4. **Monthly minimum fees:** Fees charged if your business doesn't meet the minimum required transactions.

Payment processing companies are an increasingly popular alternative to traditional merchant services accounts. Payment processing companies sometimes provide extra functionality, like accessories that let you use your phone to accept credit card payments. The fee categories that you need to consider will be similar to merchant services account fees. If you find a payment processor that you like, remember that you'll still need to connect it to a business checking account to receive payments.

Another good thing about smaller banks is that decisions are made at the branch level, which can be much quicker than big banks where decisions are made at a higher level. When choosing a bank for your business, you should ask yourself these questions:

- What is important to me?
- Do I want to build a close relationship with a bank that's willing to help me in any way possible?
- Do I want to be just another bank account like big banks will view me as?

Ultimately, choosing the right bank for your business comes down to the needs of your business. Writing down your banking needs can help narrow your focus to what you should be looking for. Schedule meetings with various banks and ask questions about how they work with small businesses to find the best bank for your business.

Determine your legal business structure.
Before you can register your company, you need to decide what kind of entity it is. Your business structure legally affects everything from how you file your taxes to your personal liability if something goes wrong. If you own the business entirely by yourself and plan to be responsible for all debts and obligations, you can register for a sole proprietorship. Be warned that this route can directly affect your personal credit.
Alternatively, a partnership, as its name implies, means that two or more people are held personally liable as business owners. You don't have to go it alone if you can find a business partner with complementary skills to your own. It's usually a good idea to add someone into the mix to help your business flourish.

If you want to separate your personal liability from your company's liability, you may want to consider forming one of several types of corporations. This makes a business a separate entity apart from its owners, and, therefore, corporations can own property, assume liability, pay taxes, enter contracts, sue and be sued like any other individual.

One of the most common structures for small businesses, however, is the limited liability corporation. This hybrid structure has the legal protections of a corporation while allowing for the tax benefits of a partnership. Corporations, especially C-corporations, are especially suitable for new businesses that plan on "going public" or seeking funding from venture capitalists in the near future. Ultimately, it is up to you to determine which type of entity is best for your current needs and future business goals. It's important to learn about the various legal business structures that are available. If you're struggling to make up your mind, it's not a bad idea to discuss the decision with a business or legal adviser.

TIME TO BAIL BEFORE THE CRASH

Starting a business is always going to be hard. If it wasn't, everyone would own a successful startup. And while it's great to give things a red-hot go, there's no shame in admitting when things just aren't working out for you and your business. A successful entrepreneur requires a certain amount of stubbornness, but it can also be the thing that stops them from letting go when they should. So, if you're an aspiring entrepreneur (or even if you've been in the business for years), Learning something new or refreshing buried information is always a great step in the right direction towards growth,

If it isn't working out as you had first thought and you find yourself and your pockets repeatedly pounding near rock bottom, you might want to consider an exit strategy. It's also a good idea to consider an exit strategy as you compile your business plan. Generating some idea of how you'll eventually exit the business forces you to look to the future. Too often, new entrepreneurs are so excited about their business and so sure everyone everywhere will be a customer that they give very little, if any, time to show the plan on leaving the business. Think about it like this, when you board an airplane, what is the first thing they show you? How to get off of it? When you go to a movie, what do they point out before the feature begins to play? Where the exits are? Your first week of kindergarten, they line up all the kids and teach them fire drills to exit the building. Too many times I have witnessed business leaders that don't have three or four pre-determined exit routes. This has led to lower company value and even destroyed family relationships.

One of the hardest decisions in an entrepreneur's life is knowing when to call it quits. While most people go into a business thinking about their measure of success, the same measure of success they don't fully define the boundaries they are willing to accept to reach it. It's not impossible to help your business become successful but the fact still remain that nearly 50 percent of businesses fail within the five years, and 96 percent of businesses fail within the first 10 years. If you knew your company was one of those 96 percent destined to fail, wouldn't those first five years have been better spent working on something that had a chance of being in the four percent? I've been on both sides of the spectrum. I was a founding employee at Esquyre INC, which is 10 years in and still going strong. My company before that folded in only five years after not being able to find its market. Obviously, if we knew at the outset that our first start-up business was going to fail, we would have never started it in the first place, or we would have at least went about structuring it differently. But with failure comes growth from learning, without failing at the things we want to achieve the most, we will find ourselves just being mediocre, instead of letting the greatest version of ourselves show. It is only through our action or inaction that they succeed or not. With that said, when it comes time to evaluate your company, you should be as analytical as possible as many people stay with their projects out of emotional attachment, instead of good old common sense.

Here are some common sense factors that you may be able to overcome:

- If there are team disputes or advisor issues.
- If you find yourself with more set-backs than finding yourself ahead.
- If you find your product or service is not selling after more than a year of pushing it.
- If you have cash flow problems.
- If you find your-self dipping into your personal account one time too often.

In my experience, these seem the most difficult, especially when you're going through them. However, you can always work through team problems with coaching or even by replacing people, and there are always ways to find money if the product or service is sound. At a few of my companies, we bootstrapped for years until we got our first big clients and/or sources of funding.

If you are not careful here are some more factors that may lead you toward shutting down prematurely:

- If the core intellectual property of your company is owned by another person or company that you don't control.
- If your company doesn't have sound structure.
- If you've been unable to find a fit for your product/service within the market after sometime, even after pivoting.
- If you have legal issues.
- And most importantly failing to pay or falling behind in your taxes.

Just a little food for thought, if your business is not your passion or focus related, and you're still at a pre-traction phase, then you may as well quit right now. After all, if you aren't passionate about your own project or the service you provide, then how can you expect your team or your customers to be?

If you answered "yes", you may have a problem. It might be a sign that it's time to think of an exit strategy. However, it could also be a sign of a problem that can be solved in a different way, a staff member to take the load off, for example. As we said above, most businesses don't become profitable until about the second or third year of business, so we usually don't advise throwing in the towel after, say, 14 months unless you are digging yourself into a hole that you won't ever recover from. However, if you're starting to feel like maybe you want out, take it seriously. Take time to analyze all options available to you, to make very sure this is the best course of action. If you do decide to close up shop, regroup, reflect, and plan for your next small business!

We should also mention here that skills training can make the difference when it comes to entrepreneurship success. No matter what stage of business you're in, small business education, like the kind offered by us at AAHC, may help you tip the balance from "What do I do?" to "I have a plan!" Here with the African American Council we believe that Knowledge is power and wisdom key towards building and leaving behind a legacy! Obviously, we want you to love what you do, but like the song says, sometimes love just ain't enough. If you've been getting that nagging feeling that maybe this particular stage of your entrepreneurship journey is at an end, one or more of these signs might sound familiar to you.

- **You're losing money at a rapid pace.** It can take up to three years for a small business to turn a profit, but if you've tried everything and still see your money slipping away faster than it's coming in, it's not good. Lack of cash flow is the number one cause of business failure.

- **Your relationships are suffering.** If you're so stressed that you're taking it out on your loved ones, or work so much that you never see them, it could also be an indication that it's time to close up shop. However, it could also be a sign that you need to hire some help!

- **You're bored.** When you started your small business, you were thrilled by it and spent every waking hour dreaming and planning. But what if you have no more ideas and are just running on fumes? Could you benefit from seeking outside help with planning or networking?

- **You dread your workdays.** If the thought of another day as a small business owner makes you feel miserable, that's not a good sign. Analyze this feeling. Would a new direction for the business help? Some new employees to take the load off? Think about what it would take to make you love your small business again, and plan out all options.

- **Your health is taking a turn for the worse.** If the pressure and stress you're feeling about your small business is taking a toll on your health, then something's not right.

If you do decide to shut down your business, here's the course of action I recommend:

Be prepared.
Gather any contracts, bank statements, legal documents, invoices and any IP, and anything else you may have and read through them carefully. Find out what your current obligations are, if any, and to whom. During the acquisition of a company I was previously involved in, the sale hit a snag because one of the creditors had a conflict of interest with the new buyer. It took months to sort and caused operations to shut down in the meantime.

Open the lines of communication.
If you have any partners or co-founders, discuss your intentions and the reasoning behind it. If you've decided to completely dissolve the company, lay out the division of ownership with supporting documents. If you've decided on a buyout, have the offer in writing. While advising one company, I found that all three co-founders had their own individual reasons for wanting to shut down, but they had not spoken to each other about it. Simply having them to discuss it with each other led to a new beginning for everything.

Be courteous.
Shut down any websites and applications you have launched, and make sure you notify any customers you may have of the end date and offer them a transition plan. After all, this likely won't be your last venture, so you want to keep them on your side. At one of my former companies, when we discontinued a game, we sent notice to the players months in advance, and gave them full, free access to the game as an open-source project. Lastly, don't quit being an entrepreneur forever. Remember to fail fast and learn from your mistakes in order to find yourself in the ranks of the successful 4 percent of business owners. Customers' perceptions of your business can really make or break a business. Deliver quality experiences and products, and

they'll quickly sing your praises on social media; mess it up, and they'll tell the world even faster. Fast growth depends on making your current and potential customers happy with their experience. Compared with large companies, small businesses are nimble, and often better able to see, anticipate and respond to their customers' needs. The most successful small businesses exploit this advantage, by bringing new and innovative products and services to market more quickly and developing and nurturing long-term customer relationships. In the early stages of your business, you'll likely see a very lean profit margin (or no profit at all), so any money you do make should go directly toward helping you grow. A startup's ability to invest in (itself) helps accelerate growth, in those early years, it's critical to make sure that you're redirecting any revenues back into the company. It's vital to invest early and heavily in order to grow quickly. While agility is an important quality for a startup, you can't fly by the seat of your pants when you're running a business. Planning your next step, even if that means anticipating all possible scenarios, is the best way to stay grounded and secure the structure of your business as your business evolves.

Small businesses run most effectively when there are systems in place. One of the most important systems for a small business is an accounting system. Your accounting system is necessary in order to create and manage your budget, set your rates and prices, conduct business with others, and file your taxes. You can set up your accounting system yourself, or a reliable accountant, don't just hire the first accountant that you see and the same goes for a manager and a lawyer, always do your research on the people that you're going to work with. But if you accountant is for taking away some of the guesswork.

Quitting something comes with a certain amount of guilt, which is pretty unavoidable. But there's absolutely no shame in walking away from something that isn't going to benefit you. While it might feel like a blow to your pride, admitting that your business is going nowhere can only open you up to future projects that have a much better potential. Success is never reached if you hold onto failure, and you'll never find out what's in store if you cling to something that is going nowhere.

HOW TO FILE YOUR OWN

Personal Taxes

Each and every year just over and over again we go through the same (sometimes seeming like a endless) process, tax season. Sure, you could get a nice tax refund. Or you could put all that hard work and time into your taxes and get barely anything. Luckily for you, we've got a few tips on how to maximize your tax return. We want to make sure that you avoid mistakes on your taxes. If you don't you might end up paying even more taxes than you have to or under-reporting your income and paying interest and penalties later. While most of us may disagree on how the government spends our taxes, at tax time, many of us are looking for ways to pay no more than we owe, or even boost our tax refunds.

We don't want that to happen. This year, follow these easy ways that can help you possibly maximize your tax return. These strategies go beyond the obvious to give you tried-and-true ways to reduce your tax liability.

The Roots of a Revolution

1. Don't Leave Money on the Table

If you forget to use all of your Flexible contributions to your individual retirement and 529 accounts, you could leave money on the table. You have until December 31 to use money in your FSA or contribute to a 529 account. Some states even allow deductions for 529 contributions. Wondering how you can maximize your next year refund? If you're ready to start working on maximizing your return for next year, consider how much you can contribute to retirement plans in this current year. You can contribute up to $19,500 to 401(k) plans. Choosing to not file a return because your income for 2019 might also mean you're leaving money on the table. Just because your income doesn't require you to file doesn't mean you're not due a refund. And if you're eligible for a refund, you have to file a return to get it.

2. Rethink your filing status

One of the first decisions you make when completing your tax return, choosing a filing status, can affect your refund's size, especially if you're married. What's your best filing status? If you have a tax preparer, make sure you update them on any life changes you've had, such as getting married or divorced. Your relationship status on December 31 determines your filing status for the entire year and is the one you need to use when filing that year's tax return. Options include:

- Single
- Head of household
- Married, filing jointly
- Married, filing separately
- Qualifying widower

Whether or not you can file head of household, which comes with some tax benefits, is one of the more confusing questions. To file as a head of household, you must:

- Be unmarried or considered unmarried on Dec. 31 of the relevant tax year
- Paid more than half of the costs associated with keeping and maintaining your home during the tax year
- Have a qualifying person, such as a child or other dependent, living with you for at least half the year

If you could technically file with two different statuses, like if you could file single and head of household, you might try calculating your taxes with both to find out which is in your best interest. This could mean checking to see if your refund changes whether you file as single or head of household or whether you file as married jointly or separately. Just don't actually file your taxes until you make a decision, as you can only file once.

While approximately 96% of married couples file jointly each year, a joint return is not always the most beneficial option.

- **Married Filing Separately.** status often requires more effort, but the time you invest can offer tax savings, under the right conditions. For example, if one spouse has a lot of medical expenses, such as COBRA payments resulting from a job loss, computing taxes individually might allow for a larger deduction.
- **The Child Tax Credit.** is available to separately filing spouses. The credit is $2,000 per child under 17 years old, and it can now be claimed by a separate filer with less than $200,000 in adjusted gross income (it's $400,000 for joint filers).

Choosing to file separate returns can have its drawbacks, such as losing certain deductions available to joint filers. You'll need to weigh this carefully to maximize your refund potential. Also, both spouses must take either the standard deduction or itemize their deduction. You can't mix-and-match between the two returns. Calculating your taxes both ways will point you in the higher refund direction. When you use TurboTax, we'll do this calculation for you and recommend the best filing status.

- This filing status enjoys a higher standard deduction and more favorable tax brackets than filing as Single.
- A qualifying dependent can be a child you supported financially and who lived with you for more than six months. Or, it can be an elderly parent you supported.
- Don't take the standard deduction if you can itemize.
- Claim your friend or relative you've been supporting.
- Take above-the-line deductions if eligible.
- Don't forget about refundable tax credits.
- Contribute to your retirement to get multiple benefits.

3. Claim All Available Deductions, Including Charitable Contributions.

Many taxpayers who care for elderly parents don't realize they can claim Head of Household status. If you provide more than half your parent's financial support, even if your parent doesn't live with you, you can file as Head of Household. If you have been supporting your friend, significant other or relative, you may be able to claim him or her as a dependent. Dig into all deductions available to you.

The Roots of a Revolution

Some of the more common deductions include charitable donations, medical costs, prepaid interest on a mortgage and education expenses. Deductions are subtracted from your adjusted gross income, which lowers your actual taxable income. Your taxable income is the amount you pay taxes on. The lower your taxable income, the less tax you pay and the higher refund you might receive. If you're charitably inclined and itemize your deductions, you can maximize your return by taking advantage of donations in all forms, cash and goods. That means you can claim the value of those clothes donated to a local church drive, for example.
Be sure to keep good records and receipts. Also, make sure that you're only claiming deductions for organizations that have tax-exempt status with the IRS.

There are some rules regarding who qualifies, but the deduction is legitimate if your non-relative has lived with you the entire year (relatives don't need to live with you), doesn't provide more than half of his or her own support and doesn't earn more than $4,200 in taxable income. Although you can no longer claim the dependent exemption under tax reform, there is a new tax credit for non-child dependents worth up to $500. Above-the-line tax deductions allow you to reduce your taxable income without itemizing. Examples include if you are a teacher and paid for your students' school supplies, went back to school to land that promotion, paid alimony in that year (if your divorce was final before that tax year), pay self-employment tax, paid student loan interest, contribute to your IRA or had unreimbursed moving expenses if you are active-duty military. The reduction to your taxable income may also help you get a bigger advanced premium tax credit if you received assistance to help pay for insurance in the health insurance marketplace.

Many deductions exist that you may not be aware of, and several of them are pretty commonly overlooked. The deductions you qualify for can make a significant difference on your tax refund. They include:

- **State sales tax** – Using the IRS's calculator, you can determine how much of your state and local sales taxes you can deduct.

- **Reinvested dividends** – This one technically isn't a deduction, but it can reduce your overall tax liability. When you automatically have dividends from mutual funds reinvested, include that in your cost basis. This way, when you sell shares, you might reduce your taxable capital gain.

- **Out-of-pocket charitable contributions** – Big donations aren't the only way to get a write-off. Keep track of the qualified small expenses too, like ingredients for the yummy cake that you donated to the bake sale. You might find yourself surprised by how quickly a few charitable expenditures here and there can add up.

- **Student loan interest** – Even if you didn't pay this yourself, you can take the deduction for it as long as you are the one who is obligated to pay. Under new guidelines, if someone else pays the loan, the IRS views it as if you were given the money and used it to pay the student loan. If you meet all of the requirements then you would be eligible for the deduction.

- **Child and dependent care** – Up to $6,000 of qualifying expenses can be used for the Child and Dependent Care Tax Credit.

- **Earned Income Tax Credit or EITC** – This credit helps families with low and moderate income levels. It's meant to benefit working families with children. If you have three or more qualifying kids, the credit could be worth up to $6,557 for you for tax year 2019, and could net you a refund even if you don't have any tax.

- **State income tax paid on last year's return** – If you paid money on your state income tax return last year, you can add that to any other state income tax, up to $10,000, and use it as an itemized deduction.

- **Certain jury duty fees** – If your company paid you while on jury duty and your employer required you to hand over your jury duty pay from the court; you can claim the amount that you handed over as an adjustment to your income.

- **Medical miles** - Subject to an overall AGI threshold for total medical expenses and worth 20 cents per mile this tax year. For this tax year, the threshold is any qualifying unreimbursed medical expenses that exceed 10% of your AGI.

- **Charity miles** - Fully deductible at 14 cents per mile in 2019. So, if you drove 50 miles per week to volunteer for a charity this tax year, that's an additional $364 deduction: 52 weeks/year x 50 miles/week = 2,600 miles you drove in a year

2,600 miles x \$0.14/mile = \$364

It's important to keep not good but spectator records for your deductions especially when you don't receive some type of receipt as with some charitable contributions and charitable or medical miles. Nothing fancy is required, even a spiral notebook in your glove compartment is fine. Make sure to keep track of:

- The date, miles and medical or charitable purpose of each trip
- The market value of any in-kind donations, such as clothing and household goods
- The dollars you spend in order to do charity work, for example, when you bake for a fundraiser the cost of your ingredients is deductible, but the value of the time you spent baking isn't

Don't Forget About Refundable Tax Credits, a tax credit is a dollar-for-dollar reduction of the tax you owe, and a refundable tax credit will allow you to have a credit beyond your tax liability. The earned income tax credit is worth up to \$6,557 for a family with three or more children. One out of five taxpayers who are eligible for the credit fails to claim it, according to the IRS. Some taxpayers miss this valuable credit because they are newly qualified due to changes in their income. Or they chose not to file their taxes if their income is below the IRS income-filing threshold ($12,200 if you're single or $24,400 if you're married filing jointly).

4. Report All Your Income

Some people fail to report all their income on their return. This oversight, intentional or not, can cost you. If you have unreported income and the IRS uncovers it, you're looking at interest and penalties for unpaid taxes. Sadly, you won't get a free pass when you make an honest mistake. So spend a few extra minutes reviewing your return. Think through the year and your accounts to make sure you don't forget any income sources. It's often 1099 income that's over-looked, things like contract work, interest income and dividends. It can be helpful to keep a spreadsheet of all of your tax information, including sources of income, 1099s, charitable gifts and IRA and 529 contributions. Update it each year to help avoid missing things during tax prep. You're less likely to forget about a 1099 if it's listed in your prior year's tax information.

You have until the filing deadline (unless it's delayed due to a weekend or holiday) to open or contribute to a traditional IRA for the previous tax year. That gives you the flexibility of claiming the credit on your return, filing early and using your refund to open the account.

- Traditional IRA contributions can reduce your taxable income. You can take advantage of the maximum contribution and, if you're at least 50 years old, the catch-up provision can add to your IRA.
- Although contributions to a Roth IRA don't give you a deduction, they still qualify for the valuable Saver's Credit if you meet income guidelines.
- If you're self-employed, you have until October 15, **of that tax year** to contribute to a certain self-employed retirement plans, provided that you timely file an extension. If you don't file for an extension, the filing deadline for that year is the deadline for most contributions.

Pre-tax contributions to a Health Savings Account (HSA) can also reduce your taxable income. You can make these up until the filing deadline as well. Certain requirements must be met in order to open and contribute to an HSA:

- You must be enrolled in a health insurance plan that has high deductibles that meet or exceed the IRS's required amounts.

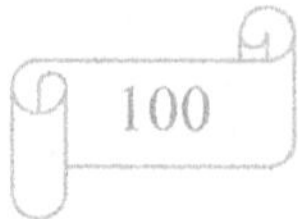

- That plan must also impose the maximum annual out-of-pocket cost ceilings that meet the IRS's limitations.

You won't be able to participate in an HSA if any of the following are true:

- You have other "first-dollar" medical coverage
- You enroll in Medicare
- You are claimed as a dependent on another taxpayer's return
-

Remember, timing can boost your tax refund
Taxpayers who watch the calendar improve their chances of getting a larger refund. Look for payments or contributions you can make before the end of the year that will reduce your taxable income. For example:

- If you can, make January's mortgage payment before **December 31** and get the added interest for your mortgage interest deduction.
- Schedule health-related treatments and exams in the last quarter of the year to boost your medical expense deduction potential.
- This could be the time to make some charitable contributions, but make sure it's a

qualified charity and be sure to keep track of your expenditures in your records.

- If you're self-employed, look at any purchases you'll need to make that can qualify for deductions, Buy things like office equipment and software before the end of the year to help boost your refund.
- If you are able to claim the home office deduction, you can even deduct the cost of painting your home office if you want to start the New Year with a fresh new look in your workspace.

Meet the Deadlines, your federal tax return must be electronically filed or postmarked by May to July, of that tax year. The only exception is if you file an extension, which must be filed or postmarked by that date. An extension buys you through mid-October to file your return without penalties. However, you will still owe interest for any tax that was owed by July 15 and not paid.

Tax credits usually work better than deductions as refund boosters because they're a dollar-for-dollar reduction of your taxes. If you get a $100 credit, you get $100 off your taxes. Many Americans leave money on the table when it comes to claiming tax credits.

The Roots of a Revolution

Let's break it down:

- Did you know that 20% of eligible Americans don't claim the Earned Income Tax Credit? If you meet the guidelines, you may be eligible for the EITC, even if you're single with no children.

- If you have no qualifying children, the maximum credit amount is $529 for that tax season.

- If you have three or more qualifying children, for the maximum credit jumps to $6,557.

- If you have kids, it also pays to claim the Child and Dependent Care Credit.

If you're a college student or supporting a child in college, you may be eligible to claim valuable education credits.

- The American Opportunity Credit is refundable up to $1,000. This means you could receive as much as $1,000, even if you don't have a tax bill. The total credit is $2,500 and applies only to funds paid towards the first four years of qualified undergraduate higher education expenses.

- If you're in graduate school or beyond, you may be eligible for the Lifetime Learning Credit. For this tax year, you can claim 20% of your qualified costs up to $10,000, or a maximum of $2,000, depending on your income.

Tax credits for energy-saving home improvements can also keep more money in your wallet throughout the year and at tax time. Turbo tax, The IRS website and Tax act are some fantastic places to do your own person taxes.

- The credit for 2019 is up to 30% of the cost of certain qualified energy expenditures. After 2019, reduced percentages apply for this tax year and the next. That means if you installed solar panels at a cost of $20,000, your total credit is $6,000 in 2019.

- Any portion unused in last year carries over to the next year.
- That carryover doesn't apply to the credit for electric vehicles, but the IRS is still offering up to $7,500 per qualifying vehicle for 2019, subject to manufacturer sales

limits. The credit begins to phase out once each manufacturer has sold more than 200,000 qualifying vehicles.

Remember, with TurboTax will ask you simple questions and fill out the right forms for you. We'll find every tax deduction and credit you qualify for to get you the biggest tax refund, guaranteed. There are ways to boost the tax refund you get back from the government. It's all about optimizing your deductions, claims and credits. Even your filing status can get you a bigger refund. If you're really trying to get the biggest refund you can, make sure that you use the best tax filing software you can. A good tax service will help you get every deduction and credit that you qualify for. It will also guide you through the process so that you don't have to feel lost or confused as you work through your return. Filing your taxes yourself has never been easier. As long as you have internet access, you can submit your tax return from the comfort of your couch. Before you get started, however, you'll have to choose which online tax software to trust with all your financial details. That's not always easy. That's where Smart Asset comes in. We reviewed the most common tax programs available. Our analysis included a breakdown and comparison of available features such as penalty and fee guarantees and audit support, as well as a price comparison.

When it comes to best overall software, in my opinion, there are two that stand out above the rest: TurboTax and Tax Act. TurboTax and Tax Act was our number one and number two choices because it offers the most features out of all the software we reviewed, and it makes tax filing about as easy as possible. You can upload your W-2 form directly to the site and you can upload it by taking a picture of it. You receive your refund through direct deposit and there is even a mobile app. The service searches over 350 tax deductions when you file to ensure you receive the deductions and applicable credits. They're very easy to use and walk you through the filing process by asking a series of questions about your financial situation. The questions are interview-style and are written in plain English. Based on your answers, the software fills out the appropriate tax forms. In terms of features, that offers free audit support and free multi-year storage.

That means if you use the program year after year, your previous returns are saved on the site, saving you time and effort. The software also has extra features, tools and calculators specifically for self-employed filers and people with more complex tax returns. For example, self-employed filers get a complimentary one-year subscription to QuickBooks Self-Employed. This services stores receipts and tracks miles traveled throughout the year to help maximize your business deductions.

Once you've snagged your bigger refund, you'll have to decide what to do with it.

- While it might be nice to treat yourself with that money, you could use it for a financial gain. For example, a smart way to use your tax refund could be using it to pay off any debts. This can include student loans, a mortgage payment or your credit card bill. If you have multiple debts, your refund could go to the loan with the highest APR. and if you paid off all of your debt or don't have any, make that refund work for you but investing it smartly and not recklessly. Every investment isn't always a good investment.

- You might also want to use your refund to start investing. A financial advisor can guide you on how to invest in a tax-efficient manner. To find a financial advisor in your area, use the Smart Asset financial advisor matching tool. After answering some questions about your goals, you'll be matched with up to three advisors in your area, and you can interview them to ensure that they're right for you.

- A third alternative is putting those funds into a savings account immediately, avoiding the urge to spend it instead. This allows your money to grow inside an FDIC-insured account, offering an ideal way to save towards a savings goal or to simply build an emergency fund.

Why EITC is Important?

The earned income tax credit, EITC (Earned Income Tax Credit,) is the federal government's largest benefit for workers. For people who have earned income from working for someone or running a business or farm, it's money that positively impacts change in their life, family and community. We know four out of five eligible taxpayers receive their EITC. This means millions of taxpayers are putting EITC dollars to work for them. But missing that one in five means millions of people are not taking advantage of this valuable credit they earned. Almost a third of those who qualify for EITC qualify for the first time this year due to changes in their marital, parental or financial status. Outreach every year is so important.

The Roots of a Revolution

Who are we missing?

We estimate that four out of five workers claim the EITC they earned. Help IRS reach the potentially qualifying workers who miss out on thousands of dollars every year on EITC. Help us educate them about the credit and motivate them to join the four out of five who file and claim it. This includes workers who are:

- living in rural areas,
- self-employed,
- receiving certain disability pensions or have children with disabilities,
- without a qualifying child,
- not proficient in English,
- grandparents raising their grandchildren, or
- recently divorced, unemployed, or experienced other changes to their marital, financial or parental status

All Workers Claiming the EITC Must:

- Have a Social Security number that is valid for employment and issued before the due date of the return (including extensions)
- Not file as married filing separate
- Not file Form 2555 or Form 2555-EZ (related to foreign earned income)
- Meet the investment income limitation

- Have earned income
- Not be the qualifying child of another person,
- Generally, be a U.S. citizen or resident alien for the entire year.

Understanding the IRS's annual threshold limits is a primary factor in determining whether or not you must file a tax return each year. Most individuals will have similar tax scenarios from year to year, which can be helpful in knowing and understanding your tax obligations. However, some people may experience drastic changes from year to year as a result of a drop in income from a lost job, a marriage, new children, or even a jump in income when moving beyond dependency or higher education. The IRS provides detailed information each year for every scenario, so the key is staying up to date on the requirements relative to your personal situation. You should always maintain a record of your returns for up to six years.

To Claim EITC With a Qualifying Child, the Child Must Pass All of the Following Tests:

- Relationship/Marriage
- A son or daughter (including an adopted child or child lawfully placed for adoption)
- Stepchild

- Foster child placed by an authorized placement agency or a court with competent jurisdiction
- Brother, sister, half brother, half sister, stepbrother, stepsister or a descendant of any of them
- Age, at the end of the filing year, the child was: Younger than the worker (or the worker's spouse if married filing jointly) and younger than 19 or, younger than 24 and a full-time student
- Any age if permanently and totally disabled Residency
- Child must live with the worker, or the worker's spouse if filing a joint return, in the United States, for more than half of the year Joint Return
- The child cannot have filed a joint return, unless the child and the child's spouse did not have a filing requirement and filed only to claim a refund.

FILING BUSINESS TAXES

The form of business you operate determines what taxes you must pay and how you pay them. The following are the five general types of business taxes. When it's time to file a federal income tax return for your small business, there are various ways you can do it, depending on whether you run the business as a sole proprietorship or use a legal entity such as an LLC or corporation. Each type of entity requires a different tax form on which you report your business income and expenses. Regardless of the form you use, you generally calculate your taxable business income in similar ways. TurboTax has two products to serve business owners, TurboTax Home & Business is designed for sole proprietors and 1099 contractors, and while TurboTax Business helps you prepare taxes for corporations, partnerships and LLCs. All businesses except partnerships must file an annual income tax return. Partnerships file an information return. The form you use depends on how your business is organized. Refer to Business Structures to find out which returns you must file based on the business entity established.

Gather all business records. Before filling out any tax form to report your business income, you should have all records in front of you that report your business earnings and expenses. If you use a computer program or a spreadsheet to organize and keep track of all transactions during the year, calculating your income and deductions is much easier than trying to remember every sale and expenditure that occurred during the year. TurboTax and Tax Act works with programs like QuickBooks and Quicken, so you can import information directly into your tax return.

Determine the correct IRS tax form. You always need to report your business earnings to the IRS and pay tax on them, but choosing the right form to report earnings on depends on how you operate your business. Many small business owners use a sole proprietorship which allows them to report all of their business income and expenses on a Schedule C attachment to their personal income tax return. If you run the business as an LLC and you are the sole owner, the IRS also allows you to use the Schedule C attachment. However, if you use a corporation or elect to treat your LLC as one, then you must always prepare a separate corporate tax return on Form 1120 (or Form 1120S if you are an S-Corp). When you use TurboTax Home & Business (sole proprietors and contractors) or TurboTax Business (corporations, LLCs and partnerships), you just need to answer simple questions about your business income and expenses, and we'll fill in all the right forms for you. The federal income tax is a pay-as-you-go tax. You must pay the tax as you earn or receive income during the year. An employee usually has income tax withheld from his or her pay. If you do not pay your tax through withholding, or do not pay enough tax that way, you might have to pay estimated tax. If you are not required to make estimated tax payments, you may pay any tax due when you file your return. For additional information refer to Publication 583. Be aware of different filing deadlines.

As a business owner, it's important to understand your federal, state, and local tax requirements. This will help you file your taxes accurately and make payments on time. The business structure you choose when starting a business will determine what taxes you'll pay and how you pay them. When you use a Schedule C, it becomes part of your Form 1040 and therefore, no separate filing deadlines apply. It is generally subject to the same April 15 deadline; however, for 2020 it is July 15 due to the corona-virus. If you are taxed as a C-Corp, you need to file a Form 1120, you must file it by the 15th day of the forth month following the close of the tax year, which for most taxpayers is April 15. If you are taxed as an S-Corp, you need to file a Form 1120S, you must file it by the 15th day of the third month following the close of the tax year, which for most taxpayers is March 15.

It's not mandatory, but most of the time people normally file their business tax return and personal income tax return together and not separate, unless their business was a corporation or they identify their LLC as a corporation. Yes it's true, you can file your personal and business taxes separately if your company is a corporation, according to the IRS, it depends on how complicated your business is and/or if you have a regular nine to five besides your business.

A corporation is a business that's seen as an entity separate from its owner or owners that pays its own tax. Corporations file their taxes using Form 1120. Limited liability companies (LLCs) can also choose to be treated as a corporation by the IRS, whether they have one or multiple owners. In that situation, they must also file their taxes using Form 1120, which means the owners must file their personal and business taxes separately. All other business structures must report their income or losses via the owner or owner's personal tax returns. We'll look at each structure's tax reporting obligations below. Need more time to file your taxes? Use tax Form 4868 or Form 7004 to apply for an extension.

Remember, when you use TurboTax or Tax Act, to prepare your taxes, they'll determine which forms you need and put the information in all the right places. All you need to do is answer simple, plain-English questions. Energy-related tax incentives can make home and business energy improvements more affordable. There are credits for buying energy efficient appliances and for making energy-saving improvements. Find out if you qualify for state, local, utility, or federal incentives.

Energy Tax Breaks by State

- Find programs and policies in your state that support renewable energy and energy efficiency. Search the Database of State Incentives for Renewable and Efficiency (DSIRE).

- Find out if your state offers a sales tax holiday on energy-efficient home appliances.

Federal Energy Tax Breaks
Energy-Saving Home Improvements
Residential Energy Credits allow savings for any of these purchases for your home:

- Solar panels
- Solar water heaters
- Wind turbines

- Geothermal heat pumps
- Fuel-cell equipment

New Energy Tax Breaks for 2018 - 2020

A new law passed in December 2019 reauthorized many energy tax breaks that had expired in 2017. They're now retroactive to 2018 and extended through 2020 or longer. They include credits for:

- Energy efficient homes
- Energy-efficient commercial buildings
- Non-business energy property
- Qualified fuel cell vehicles
- Alternative fuel vehicle refueling property
- Energy tax incentives for biodiesel and renewable diesel, extended through 2022

Small businesses can receive a tax deduction for making charitable donation (PDF, Download Adobe Reader. The IRS has specific reporting requirements when a small business donates:

- Non-food inventory
- Food
- Intellectual property

You won't receive a tax deduction for donating services. But you may be able to deduct expenses related to the donation, like travel or materials.

Generally, only the following types of organizations can be qualified organizations.
As in:

1. A community chest, corporation, trust, fund, or foundation organized or created in or under the laws of the United States, any state, the District of Columbia, or any possession of the United States (including Puerto Rico). It must, however, be organized and operated only for charitable, religious, scientific, literary, or educational purposes, or for the prevention of cruelty to children or animals. Certain organizations that foster national or international amateur sports competition also qualify.

2. War veterans organizations, including posts, auxiliaries, trusts, or foundations, organized in the United States or any of its possessions (including Puerto Rico). Domestic fraternal societies, orders, and associations operating under the lodge system. Your contribution to this type of organization is deductible only if it is to be used solely for charitable, religious, scientific, literary, or educational purposes, or for the prevention of cruelty to children or animals.

3. Certain nonprofit cemetery companies or corporations. (Your contribution to this type of

organization isn't deductible if it can be used for the care of a specific lot or mausoleum crypt.)

4. The United States or any state, the District of Columbia, a U.S. possession (including Puerto Rico), a political subdivision of a state or U.S. possession, or an Indian tribal government or any of its subdivisions that perform substantial government functions. (Your contribution to this type of organization is deductible only if it is to be used solely for public purposes.)

For example you contribute cash to your city's police department to be used as a reward for information about a crime. The city police department is a qualified organization, and your contribution is for a public purpose. You can deduct your contribution. Or you make a voluntary contribution to the social security trust fund, not earmarked for a specific account. Because the trust fund is part of the U.S. government, you contributed to a qualified organization. You can deduct your contribution.

Take for example:
- Manufacture or sell certain products.
- Operate certain kinds of businesses.
- Use various kinds of equipment, facilities, or products.

- Receive payment for certain services.

Form 720 - The federal excise taxes reported on Form 720, consist of several broad categories of taxes, including the following.

- Environmental taxes.
- Communications and air transportation taxes.
- Fuel taxes.
- Tax on the first retail sale of heavy trucks, trailers, and tractors.
- Manufacturers taxes on the sale or use of a variety of different articles

Form 2290 - There is a federal excise tax on certain trucks, truck tractors, and buses used on public highways. The tax applies to vehicles having a taxable gross weight of 55,000 pounds or more. Report the tax on Form 2290. For additional information, see the instructions for Form 2290.

Form 730 - If you are in the business of accepting wagers or conducting a wagering pool or lottery, you may be liable for the federal excise tax on wagering. Use Form 730, to figure the tax on the wagers you receive.

Form 11-C - Use Form 11-C, Occupational Tax and Registration Return for Wagering, to register for any wagering activity and to pay the federal occupational tax on wagering. Excise tax has several general excise tax programs. One of the major components of the excise program is motor fuel. For additional information, refer to Excise Taxes.

THE VALUE OF CD AND TRUST ACCOUNTS

How Does a CD Work?

You may ask, how does a CD actually work? Well, opening a CD is very similar to opening any standard bank deposit account. The difference is what you're agreeing to when you sign on the dotted line (even if that signature is now digital). After you've shopped around and identified which CD(s) you'll open, completing the process will lock you into a four things. Certificates of Deposit (CD) are useful for people looking for a way to save money while earning a relatively high interest. This not only helps you save money, but also earns you interest without requiring any effort on your part. The disadvantages of CD's are minor and typically outweighed by their advantages. Once your CD is established and funded, the bank or credit union will administer it like most other deposit accounts, with either monthly or quarterly statement periods, paper or electronic statements, and usually monthly or quarterly interest payments deposited to your CD balance, where the interest will compound.

Although it may not be on your radar, consider the benefits of a Certificate of Deposit (CD). In a nutshell, it is a deposit account with a set term, typically running anywhere from three months to 10 years. But more than that, a CD is designed to increase your savings because regardless of what the market does, money you put into a certificate of deposit grows thanks to its superpower: interest. Almost all consumer financial institutions offer them, although it's up to each bank which CD terms it wants to offer, how much higher the rate will be compared to the bank's savings and money market products, and what penalties it applies for early withdrawal.

- **The interest rate:** Locked rates are a positive in that they provide a clear and predictable return on your deposit over a specific time period. The bank cannot later change the rate and therefore reduce your earnings. On the flip side, a fixed return may hurt you if rates later rise substantially and you've lost your opportunity to take advantage of higher-paying CDs.

- **The term:** This is the length of time you agree to leave your funds deposited to avoid any penalty (e.g., 6-month CD, 1-year CD, 18-month CD, etc.) The term ends on the "maturity date," when your CD has fully matured and you can withdraw your funds penalty-free.

- **The principal:** With the exception of some specialty CDs, this is the amount you agree to deposit when you open the CD.

- **The institution:** The bank or credit union where you open your CD will determine aspects of the agreement, such as early withdrawal penalties (EWPs) and whether your CD will be automatically reinvested if you don't provide other instructions at the time of maturity.

Shopping around is crucial to finding the best CD rates because different financial institutions offer a surprisingly wide range. Your brick-and-mortar bank might pay a pittance on even long-term CDs, for example, while an online bank or local credit union might pay three to five times the national average. Meanwhile, some of the best rates come from special promotions, occasionally with unusual durations such as 13 or 21 months, rather than the more common terms based on 3, 6, or 18 months or full-year increments.

1. CDs can be a safe choice

Are you skittish about betting on the stock market or tying up your money in more volatile products such as bonds? A benefit of a certificate of deposit is that it can lay many of those fears to rest. That's because the FDIC insures CDs up to the maximum allowed by law. Before you open a certificate of deposit, confirm that your financial institution is FDIC insured so if it were to fail, you know your money is protected. While having the FDIC on your side helps, CDs come with further protections. One of the main benefits of a CD is that unlike stocks, where it's possible to gain or lose large sums all in one day of trading, money put into a CD will continue to grow predictably. A CD can be secure because in some cases, you can cash out and still get the principal. However, while your initial deposit can be safe, if you cash out early, you may face an early withdrawal penalty that could eat into your interest. At times, these penalties could also impact your principal.

2. CDs can have fixed rates for fixed terms

Financial markets can be volatile and returns for investments in the stock market or real estate, for example, can be unpredictable. Some years are fruitful and others are less so. But another benefit of a CD is that you can lock in a fixed interest rate for the life of the product. Unlike the sometimes roller coaster fluctuations of the markets, a CD grows dependably courtesy of slow, steady interest. When you weigh the benefits of a certificate of deposit, there are three interest rate options to consider:

- A fixed-rate CD has a set interest rate that is paid throughout the life of the CD. A 5-year CD with a 2.00% APY (annual percentage yield) will earn that rate for the entire term, regardless of any interest rate increases or decreases during the time you have the CD.

- A variable-rate CD typically pays a percentage according to the difference between the interest rates at the beginning and end of your CD's term. For example, if you opened a 2-year variable-rate CD at 1.05% APY and it grew to 1.15% APY, your return would be calculated based on the increase over that time period.

- An adjustable-rate CD has a set interest rate at the time of your deposit but comes with the option to "adjust" the rate during the CD's term (you may only be able to adjust the rate a limited number of times). Although they are less liquid, an important CD benefit is the fixed interest. If you opt for a longer-term CD, such as one with a 3- to-5-year term, the interest rate could be higher, Depending on the financial institution where you open your account, and how long you want to keep your money in a CD, it is possible to find rates advantageous for both short and long terms.

3. CDs come with different maturity dates

Have you dreamed about soon taking the trip of a lifetime, or are you saving for something further out, like higher education for a child just learning the multiplication tables? Among the key CD benefits is that it can provide a safe place to park your funds for a set period that's aligned with your financial goals. A benefit of a CD is that it can help you save for large, one-time expenses. If, for example, you plan to take a costly vacation in the future, you can put your funds in a CD that matures right before you leave. You can match your CD to the timing of life events.

4. CDs may have low or no fees

Another benefit of a certificate of deposit is that it may have a low-to-no fee structure. Some banks don't charge a monthly fee to hold your money in a CD. This comes in handy, because you don't have to worry about fees impacting your CD earnings. While the absence of a monthly fee is a key CD benefit, it's important to remember that there could be other costs associated with a certificate of deposit. One example is the early withdrawal penalty (remember this?). Should you take your money out of the account before its maturity date, the bank may impose a penalty, which could negatively impact your interest or principal.

How Much Do CDs Pay?

While the national average is a good indicator of the direction of rates, and how much they've changed over a period of time, they are not what you should consider when shopping for CDs. Instead, look for the top nationally available rates, which stand far above industry averages.

Take one-year CDs, for instance. The current national average is just 0.21% annual percentage yield (APY). Today's top-paying institution, however, will pay you 1.20% APY on that same one-year commitment, that's five times as much. Similarly, for three-year CDs, you can currently earn 1.40% APY instead of the industry average of 0.34% APY. If you have cash you can park for a period of time, but want to earn more than the best savings and money market accounts will net you, our research on the best nationally available rates in every major CD term can lead you to maximum returns. Keep in mind that CD yields are still considered taxable as interest income on both the state and federal levels, which will impact the total return you can realize.

What Is a CD Ladder and Why Should I Build One?

The Roots of a Revolution

Smart CD investors have a specific tactic for hedging against rate changes over time and maximizing their return. It's called a certificate of deposit (CD) ladder and it enables you to access the higher rates offered by 5-year CD terms, but with the twist that a portion of your money becomes available every year, rather than every 5 years. Here's how to do it.

At the outset, you take the amount of money you want to invest in CDs and divide it by five. You then put one-fifth of the funds into a top-earning 1-year CD, another fifth into a top 2-year CD, another into a 3-year CD, and so forth through a 5-year CD. Let's say you have $25,000 available. That would give you five CDs of varying length, each with a value of $5,000. Then, when the first CD matures in a year, you take the resulting funds and open a top-rate 5-year CD. A year later, your initial 2-year CD will mature, and you'll invest those funds into another 5-year CD. You continue doing this every year with whichever CD is maturing, until you end up with a portfolio of five CDs all earning 5-year APYs, but with one of them maturing every 12 months, keeping your money a bit more accessible than if all of it were locked up for a full five years.

What Is Considered a Good Rate for a CD

The Roots of a Revolution

What makes CDs attractive as an investment vehicle is not their rate of return but their risk-free nature. When you open a CD, you know upfront exactly what interest rate you will earn and for how long. Except for some specialty CDs, the rate on your certificate is guaranteed and locked for the full duration of the certificate, meaning your return is predictable and safe. Adding to their risk-free nature is the fact that CDs, like other bank and credit union deposit products, are federally insured against bank failures. Depending on the financial institution offering them, CDs are insured by either the Federal Deposit Insurance Corporation (FDIC) or the National Credit Union Administration (NCUA).

CD minimums can run as low as $250 or $500, and you'll find plenty of options with minimums up to $1,000. As for durations, the majority of CDs carry terms of six months to five years, though shorter and longer certificates exist at some banks. Larger deposits and longer terms typically earn higher interest rates, though promotional certificates often break that general rule. The interest rates available on the best-paying CDs are usually in line with the current inflation rate, so virtually any rate higher than that is a good deal. Often, online banks and credit unions offer the best CD rates.

Maximizing Your CD Rate of Return

The Roots of a Revolution

One of the best strategies for earning as much as you can from a CD investment is to diligently shop around for the top rates. After that, the next most important strategy is to keep the funds invested for the CD's full term, so as to avoid incurring an early withdrawal penalty that will reduce your earnings. But unexpected things happen in life, and you may find yourself having no choice but to cash in a CD early. Because of that possibility, you'll be well-served by paying attention to the early withdrawal penalties of different CDs you're considering, before you make your final commitment. It's also useful, when comparing two CDs that are fairly similar, to check their compounding periods. The advantage of having interest calculated and compounded more frequently adds up over time, so look to avoid CDs that offer only annual compounding.

What Is Compound Interest?

Compound interest (or compounding interest) is interest calculated on the initial principal, which also includes all of the accumulated interest from previous periods on a deposit or loan. This is a thought that have originated in 17th century Italy, compound interest can be thought of as "interest on interest," and will make a sum grow at a faster rate than simple interest, which is calculated only on the principal amount. The rate at which compound interest accrues depends on the frequency of compounding, such that the higher the number of compounding periods, the greater the compound interest. Thus, the amount of compound interest accrued on $100 compounded at 10% annually will be lower than that on $100 compounded at 5% semi-annually over the same time period. Since the interest-on-interest effect can generate increasingly positive returns based on the initial principal amount, it has sometimes been referred to as the "miracle of compound interest," is interest that works for you instead of against you. You see you should think of your money like you're personality, if you want to change or what your finances to change you must first start with yourself. The First change you need is constant education, starting with learning:

- Compound interest (or compounding interest) is interest calculated on the initial principal, which also includes all of the accumulated interest from previous periods on a deposit or loan.

- Interest can be compounded on any given frequency schedule, from continuous to daily to annually.

- When calculating compound interest, the number of compounding periods makes a significant difference.

Growth of Compound Interest

Using the above example, since compound interest also takes into consideration accumulated interest in previous periods, the interest amount is not the same for all three years, as it would be with simple interest. While the total interest payable over the three-year period of this loan is $1,576.25. Compound interest is calculated by multiplying the initial principal amount by one plus the annual interest rate rose to the number of compound periods minus one. The total initial amount of the loan is then subtracted from the resulting value. (Where P = Principal, i = nominal annual interest rate in percentage terms, and n = number of compounding periods.) Take a three-year loan of $10,000 at an interest rate of 5% that compounds annually. What would be the amount of interest? In this case, it would be: $10,000 $[(1 + 0.05)^3 - 1]$ = $10,000 $[1.157625 - 1]$ = $1,576.25.

When calculating compound interest, the number of compounding periods makes a significant difference. The basic rule is that the higher the number of compounding periods, the greater the amount of compound interest.

The Roots of a Revolution

While CDs are traditionally a fixed-rate
investment, variable-rate CDs do exist. If you think
interest rates are likely to rise significantly, you can
benefit from a certificate whose interest rate is
adjusted during the term of the CD. These
certificates are sometimes called "raise your rate" or
"step up" CDs. Meanwhile, indexed or structured
CDs offer you the chance to earn a percentage of
the return on a stock index or commodity index.
This can result in a much higher return than a
traditional CD's, but for a trade-off of much more
risk. What Is a Variable-Rate Certificate of Deposit
(CD)?

A variable-rate certificate of deposit (CD) is a
product offered by banks and credit unions that has
a fixed term but a fluctuating interest rate. Several
factors determine this CD's rate, such as the prime
rate, the consumer price index (CPI), treasury bills,
or a market index. The basis for the amount paid
out is on a percentage difference between the
beginning index and the final index. The Federal
Deposit Insurance Corporation (FDIC) protects
variable-rate and other CDs.

- A variable-rate certificate of deposit (CD) is
  a financial instrument with a fixed term and
  a fluctuating interest rate that is based on an

assortment of factors, from the prime rate to consumer price indexes to market indexes.

- Typically, there is a penalty associated with early withdrawal of funds in a CD.

- Variable-rate CDs are most profitable during times of low interest rates, though prolonged low rates can adversely affect returns.

Understanding a Variable-Rate CD

A variable-rate CD allows investors to put their money into a secure, protected account where it will earn a relatively modest amount of interest over the life of its term. The earned interest is usually inaccessible to the account holder until the CD matures. Some issuers do offer a penalty-free CD that allows for the early withdrawal of funds. However, the interest rate is likely to be lower than CDs that do not provide this option.

A variable-rate CD pays an interest rate that can go up and down throughout the life of the security. The exact factors that will determine the interest rate of a variable-rate CD will vary depending on the institution. In contrast, a fixed-rate CD has a "locked in" interest rate with a basis from CD origination. This means the rate remains the same throughout the entire term. A CD is generally considered to be one of the safer ways to invest your money, especially as the FDIC protection backs most of them. CDs overall are among the most reliable, low-risk investment options available. They appeal to conservative, risk-averse savers and investors. Investing in CDs is also an excellent way to diversify the risk of your portfolio. For new or cautious investors, a fixed-rate CD may be the preferable place to start, but those who are comfortable increasing the risk just a little bit may want to consider a variable-rate CD.

Trust funds were once associated with high net worth individuals as a way to pass money to their heirs or charitable organizations. But trusts are fast becoming a popular tool for everyone, wealthy or not, as a solution in their estate planning. Many people have heard of trust funds, but don't understand the process of establishing one, or think that's its unbearably complex. This overview will give you an idea of the broad process of how a trust fund is set up and the kind of information you'll need. Trust funds are legal arrangements that allow individuals to place assets in a special account to benefit another person or entity. Trust funds can be complex and often require the assistance of an attorney to set up, though there are online tools for the do-it-yourselfer. The different types of trusts available include revocable or irrevocable trusts, and living or testamentary trusts, which is based on a will.

Reasons for creating a trust fund

A main reason for creating a trust is to control who receives your assets. You can assign assets through a trust during your lifetime or after death. For instance, you may want your trust fund to provide for a family member's education, or to help with the purchase of a first home. A trust can also lower your estate taxes and help you avoid probate, the legal process that requires someone to prove a will is valid.

The process for setting up a trust depends on several things: the type of trust you want, your assets and the beneficiaries. To determine the right trust for you, first identify the reason you want to set up a trust, then the beneficiary. For instance, if you decide you want to help pay the college expenses of a grandchild, an educational trust would be recommended. On the other hand, if you want a straightforward, cost-efficient method for passing your assets to your family after you die, a revocable living trust might be the best option. This type allows you to change or amend the trust anytime during your lifetime. From there, choose how you want your trust's assets to be managed and dispersed. Designate a trustee or group of trustees, such as an attorney or trusted relatives, who will uphold the purpose of the trust and handle and distribute the funds according to your wishes. For a living trust, you can assign yourself as a trustee. Decide how you want the funds distributed, such as in a lump sum at a certain date, or in specific amounts paid out at regular intervals: monthly, yearly, bi-annually, etc.

Different types of assets

The next step is to choose the amount and type of funds to move into your trust. Trust funds can consist of a range of assets, including such items as cash, real estate, stocks, bonds, artworks, classic cars, collectibles and family heirlooms. You can place these assets into the trust at once, or make a series of additions and deposits over time.

This is where trusts can become complicated, and where an attorney's help could pay off. Transferring securities and holdings from different financial institutions into your trust, which may be held separately, typically requires a lot of paperwork and expertise to avoid errors. After your assets are moved and the trust is funded, set up an investment plan that will allow those assets to grow for as long as they remain in the trust. If you have a variety of assets and stipulations in your trust, consulting an attorney may be a worthwhile investment to ensure its set up smoothly and free of mistakes.

The Roots of a Revolution

No matter your financial situation, setting up a trust for retirement is an excellent financial tool for ensuring your estate and beneficiaries are well served. Use our tools and calculators to get help making the right financial choices for your situation.

Alternatives to CDs or a Trust

If you aren't looking to lock your money up for a phase of time and want easier access to it, you could look at opening a high-yield savings account as an alternative. It should be noted that unlike a CD, where your rate is locked in, with a high-yield savings account the bank or credit union can change your rate at any time.

TRUST ACCOUNT

What Is Trust Accounting?

At its most basic level, Trust Accounting is simply bookkeeping of trust accounts in accordance with state requirements. These requirements vary from state to state, but they have a few rules in common. Namely, there is to be no comingling of client funds with the lawyer or law firm's funds, and maintaining accurate records is a must. Trust Accounting has some very specific recordkeeping requirements, which are used to maintain accurate information for both the attorney and the client. Trust Accounting requires:

- Tracking of all deposits and disbursements made through the account.

- A detailed ledger that notes every monetary transaction for each particular client.

- An account journal for each account, tracking each transaction through the account.

- Monthly reconciliation of the account.

While many people have heard about trust funds, not everyone knows that you don't have to be a billionaire to set up one and ensure your money is spent wisely. As a way of ensuring that your money is bequeathed to a loved one and can provide financial security either while you are alive or after you have passed on, a trust can be a useful estate planning tool. By law, if a person under 18 years of age inherits money, it has to be deposited in the Guardian's Fund. This restricts the investment options and flexibility that the testator might prefer, so it is thus advisable to make provision in one's will for a trust to be set up if any of your children are under 18 at the time of your death. To protect assets from creditors as they can't generally lay claim to a trust's assets. To limit future estate duty liability, if a trust fund grows from R200 000 to R1.2 million over 15 years, the growth in the trust's name could avoid the estate duty cost of 20% upon the founder's death if the assets had been held in his name. This would amount to a R200 000 saving in death taxes. Income tax planning and the conduit principle, this principle means that if the trust earns income and distributes it all to the beneficiaries, then it will not incur any tax liability on the income it earned. This tax liability passes to the beneficiary who received the taxable income.

Subject to certain tax law limitations, the trust can thus operate like a funnel through which the taxable earnings flow. The trustees of a discretionary trust may thus be able to channel taxable income to the children to reduce the overall family's tax bill.

A trust company or attorney can assist in setting up a trust fund, which is then registered with the office of the Master of the High Court. The trust needs to be registered with SARS for tax purposes and a bank account opened. Setting up and running a trust does cost money. The set-up cost could be around R7 500 and the annual fee could be a similar amount if an independent trustee is hired, which is advisable. Thus, the benefit needs to outweigh these initial and annual costs. Trusts are not only for the super rich, but the cost/benefit trade-off means that it can be too expensive to run for smaller capital amounts. In special cases (as opposed to estate duty savings alone), the founder may be prepared to incur the higher relative cost on smaller capital amounts to achieve their objectives with the trust.

Keeping the trust account safe and secure involves good business practices in the agency, understanding cyber security risks, selecting ethical and honest employees to work in the agency, and finally the agency licensee closely supervising the trust account transactions. Avoiding the appearance of impropriety: Keeping trust funds separated from firm funds A lawyer trust account is essentially a business checking account or its equivalent, established by the firm to hold client funds.

The Roots of a Revolution

Funds deposited into a trust account are neither the guardians property, lawyers property, nor if your firm's depending on the jurisdiction, a law-firm must adhere to one of two standards: Maintain a single account to hold all client funds or property, with the lawyer responsible for keeping up with fund ownership. Keep individual trust bank accounts so that one client's funds are not commingled with another's. No matter which scenario is mandated, it's only under the very rarest of circumstances that client funds may be commingled with a lawyer's business funds. In the vast majority of cases, client funds must be deposited into a separate attorneys' trust checking account and designated as such. Trust account funds may not be utilized by the law firm until they are earned. This further ensures accurate recordkeeping, as well as the integrity of the firm.

There are very strict processes and procedures outlined in the agent legislation for managing these trust funds, including accounting to clients or customers. It is essential to remember the trust account money belongs to other people. Removing money from the trust account for a reason other than one that is lawful and appropriate is a criminal offence. If an agent or person misappropriates money, the correct term is "defalcation" of trust monies; it can lead to the loss of their license as well as a prison sentence. Many small or even medium-sized businesses would never think of keeping trust funds separate from their operating accounts. They may instead develop their own system when it comes to tracking and paying for a variety of expenses throughout the year. But an insurance agency is normally dealing with extremely large sums of money, and they often don't have this luxury. Even a tiny agency may be working with millions on a regular basis. Having a way of monitoring a trust fund by tracking the commission figures isn't just nice to have, it's a necessity to properly divide, categorize, and manage earmarked funds. Without accurate reporting, agencies can end up being accused of fraud or insolvency by any of their partners (or the IRS.)

Trust money must be kept separate from the agent's general operating account, and trust money is not available to be used for the payment of the debts of the licensee or their staff. A real estate agent's good reputation is one of its biggest and most important assets. A good reputation ensures the confidence and trust of all the stakeholders in the agency such as clients, customers, suppliers, investors, regulators and employees. This confidence ensures ongoing profitability and creates increased opportunities to grow the business. Trust account management to people who aren't familiar with principles behind it will often look extraordinarily fussy. The amount of detail and precision may even seem like a waste of time. But considering funds are supposed to be tracked at the policy level, agencies can't afford to take any chances. The balance of the trust account is supposed to be at or above the level of the net premium, or else the agency may be declared insolvent. If one premium payment accidentally gets used to settle another premium from a different carrier, agencies will be liable for these mistakes eventually.

Trust funds were once associated with high net worth individuals as a way to pass money to their heirs or charitable organizations. But trusts are fast becoming a popular tool for everyone, wealthy or not, as a solution in their estate planning. Many people have heard of trust funds, but don't understand the process of establishing one, or think that's its unbearably complex. This overview will give you an idea of the broad process of how a trust fund is set up and the kind of information you'll need. Trust funds are legal arrangements that allow individuals to place assets in a special account to benefit another person or entity. Trust funds can be complex and often require the assistance of an attorney to set up, though there are online tools for the do-it-yourselfer. The different types of trusts available include revocable or irrevocable trusts, and living or testamentary trusts, which is based on a will.

Reasons for creating a trust fund

A main reason for creating a trust is to control who receives your assets. You can assign assets through a trust during your lifetime or after death. For instance, you may want your trust fund to provide for a family member's education, or to help with the purchase of a first home. A trust can also lower your estate taxes and help you avoid probate, the legal process that requires someone to prove a will is valid.

The process for setting up a trust depends on several things: the type of trust you want, your assets and the beneficiaries. To determine the right trust for you, first identify the reason you want to set up a trust, then the beneficiary. For instance, if you decide you want to help pay the college expenses of a grandchild, an educational trust would be recommended. On the other hand, if you want a straightforward, cost-efficient method for passing your assets to your family after you die, a revocable living trust might be the best option. This type allows you to change or amend the trust anytime during your lifetime. From there, choose how you want your trust's assets to be managed and dispersed. Designate a trustee or group of trustees, such as an attorney or trusted relatives, who will uphold the purpose of the trust and handle and distribute the funds according to your wishes. For a living trust, you can assign yourself as a trustee. Decide how you want the funds distributed, such as in a lump sum at a certain date or in specific amounts paid out at regular intervals: monthly, yearly, bi-annually, etc.

Different types of assets

The next step is to choose the amount and type of funds to move into your trust. Trust funds can consist of a range of assets, including such items as cash, real estate, stocks, bonds, artworks, classic cars, collectibles and family heirlooms. You can place these assets into the trust at once, or make a series of additions and deposits over time.

This is where trusts can become complicated, and where an attorney's help could pay off. Transferring securities and holdings from different financial institutions into your trust, which may be held separately, typically requires a lot of paperwork and expertise to avoid errors. After your assets are moved and the trust is funded, set up an investment plan that will allow those assets to grow for as long as they remain in the trust. If you have a variety of assets and stipulations in your trust, consulting an attorney may be a worthwhile investment to ensure its set up smoothly and free of mistakes. No matter your financial situation, setting up a trust for retirement is an excellent financial tool for ensuring your estate and beneficiaries are well served. Use our tools and calculators to get help making the right financial choices for your situation.

An agency that's ready to make some major moves has to have their finances in order before they even consider courting buyers or wooing sellers. Whether acquiring or relinquishing, clean financial records will make the due diligence process much easier for everyone involved. Having an intermediary to help you either buy or sell can be the best way to get the advice and help you need to get your trust accounts back to a manageable level. Better trust account management is also one of the best ways to ensure that money is being collected and spent as wisely as possible.

Trust Accounting Tools

Keeping track of client trusts is no easy feat, especially if you manage several client trusts. Each one needs to be managed and tracked independently and must have a full paper trail so there can never be a question that funds were used improperly. Rather than rely on manual tracking or generic accounting software, more and more lawyers are turning to legal trust accounting software, like that offered by Cosmo-Lex, Mile-High Estate planning and many more to help them manage their fiduciary duties as they relate to trusts. The risks that come with the improper management of trust funds are high; lawyers have been known to lose their licenses over what boils down to bad record-keeping. Cosmo-Lex's cloud-based trust software for attorneys makes it simple to identify and keep track of funds that are placed in trust accounts.

Funds That May Be Found In A Trust
Only certain type of funds can be placed into a trust account. These include:

- **Settlement Funds** such as those obtained through a Personal Injury case or a Real Estate transaction.

- **Unearned Income** refers to monies paid to the lawyer or law firm before services have been rendered. Fees, Cost Advances, and Retainers are all examples of unearned income.

- **Advances for Costs** are similar to unearned income, except they are to be used specifically for costs associated with managing the case.

- **Judgment Funds**, similar to settlement funds, are awarded by the court.

- **Third-Party Funds** such as those obtained from the sale of client property or monies that are to be paid to a third-party for services rendered.

Funds That Should Never Be In A Trust Account

- **Personal Funds**. This goes against the most important principle of Trust Accounting no comingling of funds. Personal funds should never be put into a client's trust account. Personal includes funds used by the law firm itself. Nothing should go into the trust account unless it is provided by or to be paid to the client.

- **Earned Income**. Wages and other money earned should never be placed into the trust account. The trust account should only have money that the client provided specifically for designated purposes.

- **Payroll**. Lawyers should never use a client trust account to manage payroll. Again, going back to the no comingling of funds rule, there should never be a reason for a law firm's payroll function to access a client trust. Payroll should come out of the firm's Operating Account.

Knowing the rules for fees earned in advance: When in doubt, go with the trust account Fees earned in advance can create a very slippery slope for law firms. When in doubt, put client retainer funds into your properly maintained attorney trust account. In limited circumstances, some jurisdictions may permit a law firm to deposit money paid by a client in advance into the firm's operating account.

Take for example; the New York Rules of Professional Conduct do not mandate what a lawyer should do with retainer funds paid in advance of legal fees, although there are ethical opinions providing guidance. New. York. State Bar Opinion 570 (1985) noted that the drafters of the Code of Professional Responsibility did not consider advance payments of fees to be client funds necessitating their deposit in a trust account. The opinion observed that Normally, when one pays in advance for services to be rendered or property to be delivered, ownership of the funds passes upon payment, absent an express agreement that the payment be held in trust or escrow, and notwithstanding the payee's obligation to perform or to refund the payment. The lawyers who drafted the Code should not lightly be assumed to have overlooked these fundamental principles in choosing the language of DR 9-102(A) .

Record keeping and accounts

This involves recordings of:

- All money coming into the trust, e.g. additions to settlement, income, gains.

- All money coming out of the trust, e.g. tax, appointments of income to beneficiaries, advancements of capital, loans, trustees' expenses.

- Minutes of trustees' meetings, resolutions etc.

- Correspondence with beneficiaries etc
- Investment policy, review of investments
- Appointments of agents/delegates
- Preparation of trust accounts

The list is not exhaustive; obviously it will depend on the circumstances of each trust. Of the above list, two are particularly important; Trustees are under a legal obligation to produce an account of the funds under their control. Of course, having proper accounts is also a matter of sound practice and necessary to ensure that all the trust assets are properly accounted for and that correct tax returns can be made in respect of the trust assets. Accounts should be prepared on each anniversary of the trust creation and it would make sense to coincide the preparation of the accounts with receipts of the annual statements relating to the trust investments.

One of the most important distinctions for accounting purposes is that between income and capital. It would generally be advisable to keep an income account and a capital account. The reasons for this will be twofold: first, for tax purposes and, second, to ensure the correct allocation of trust benefits amongst the trust beneficiaries: in many trusts there will be a beneficiary entitled to income but not to capital. As is well known, the type of trust, and therefore its taxation, depends on the treatment of the income and capital in the trust.

Although the above may seem perfectly straightforward, in fact many trustees appear to be confused as to the nature of certain payments, particularly when it comes to distributions of withdrawals from investment bonds. These are not infrequently paid to life tenants as profits "income" when, of course, bond withdrawals are capital. Some responsibility for this state of affairs must be attributed to some life offices and advisers who often do refer to such payments, often within the 5% annual allowances, as proceeds "income". This is not only factually incorrect but may in fact result in some untoward tax consequences, in some cases with capital payments being taxed as income.

Understand the difference between a trust and a will. The most significant difference between a trust and a will is that a trust allows the property to be distributed to the beneficiaries without having to go through probate. In addition, trusts are usually more private than wills. A trust, however, cannot name guardians for children. Also, a trust cannot designate how taxes and debt are to be handled. Therefore, those who set up trusts also write wills. Remember to establish the nature of the trust. Choose from a variety of trust structures to perform different functions. The kind of trust you set up depends on the type of property and assets you want it to hold and the circumstances surrounding the beneficiaries you designate. In addition, trusts can be living (which means coming into effect during your lifetime) or testamentary (coming into effect upon your death). Trusts can also be revocable, meaning you can change the terms of the trust, or irrevocable, which means the trust cannot be changed.

- A living trust can distribute assets to beneficiaries after your death or use assets to provide for your long term care while you are still alive if necessary.

- With a revocable trust, you retain some ownership of the assets in the trust, allowing you to make changes in the way the assets are handled if you deem it necessary. With an irrevocable trust, you transfer complete ownership of the assets to the trust. Revocable and irrevocable trusts also have different tax implications. Revocable trusts are subject to some estate taxes, whereas irrevocable trusts may be set up to avoid estate taxes.

- A bypass trust is useful for married couples with assets in excess of $5 million. It allows them to avoid some estate taxes when passing inheritances to heirs. A bypass trust is also known as a credit shelter trust, a marital trust, or a family trust.

- A special needs trust provides for a disabled person.

- A spendthrift trust defines the terms under which the beneficiary can receive the property, such as at a specific age or as a series of payments over a number of years. It may also limit the types of expenses on which the money can be spent, such as college tuition.

- A charitable remainder trust donates assets to a charity upon your death.

Step by step guide

List the beneficiaries. Choosing beneficiaries requires careful consideration of the amount of property to be distributed and the person's ability to manage the money responsibly. Trusts can be set up to provide for children so they can enjoy the same lifestyle they had while you were alive. It can also protect your assets from their creditors. You can distribute property equally to all beneficiaries or leave unequal amounts to each.

Appoint a trustee. The trustee's job is to manage the trust and all of its assets. The trustee must abide by all of the rules of the trust and follow any applicable state laws. You can be the trustee of your own trust, or you can appoint your adult children, other relatives, a trustworthy friend or a corporate trustee such as a bank.

- If you appoint yourself as the trustee, you should also name a successor to take over as trustee upon your death or if you become incapacitated.

- If you choose an individual to be your trustee or successor trustee, choose someone whom you trust to manage the assets responsibly and to respect your wishes. You can also nominate joint or successor trustees.

- When choosing a trustee, consider the value of the assets and the complexity of the trust. Choose someone who has the capabilities and the time to manage the responsibilities.

- If you choose a bank to be your trustee, you may also appoint an individual co-trustee.

- The advantages of having a bank as a trustee include professional record keeping and tax preparation, objectivity, no conflicts of interests and protection against misappropriation of funds.

- Disadvantages of using a bank as a trustee include the lack of a relationship with the beneficiaries, meaning they may not understand the dynamics and relationships within the family. Bank investments are also generally conservative, which may have a negative impact on the trust's potential to earn income.

- Banks do charge fees for acting as a trustee, but an individual may also expect to be paid a fee for serving as a trustee.

Notify beneficiaries of the terms of the trust and who the trustee is or will be. Generally, the trustee notifies the beneficiaries that he is in charge of the trust. He also explains when they can expect to receive the property and assets from the trust and under what conditions.

- Some states require that the trustee use specific language to do this. Others allow a trustee to use his own words.

- Most states impose a time limit within which trustees must make contact with beneficiaries upon the grantor's death.

List the assets used to fund the trust. Assets used to fund a trust include income-bearing or cash assets. Other funding sources include stocks, bonds, and real estate, as well as intangible property and life insurance policies. Funding the trust is the process of transferring ownership of the assets from you to the trust. The titles of your assets are physically changed from your name to the name of the trust. For stocks, bonds and other assets with listed beneficiaries, the beneficiary becomes the trust.

- Note that transfers from living persons will be subject to gift taxes.

Create a trust document made easy. First, the trust document contains all of the information about your trust. It explains what kind of trust you want to set up, names the trustee and beneficiaries and transfers assets to the trust fund. You can have an estate attorney draw up the trust document or you can do it on your own. After you write the document, it must be signed in front of a notary. Secondly, file the document with the state if you are required to do so. Some states require you to file trust documents with the state so there is a legal record of it. An attorney can advise you about whether or not this is necessary and how to do it. If you decide to use an attorney, find a trust and estates attorney who regularly handles matters that match your concerns and situation. For example, if you are setting up a trust for a disabled child, find an attorney who frequently deals with that area. If you don't already

know an attorney, you can search for one on sites such as:
Find Law, Find a lawyer.com or Lawyers.com.

Look for a trust and estates attorney who is a member of the American College of Trust and Estate Counsel. You can create a trust document on your own without an attorney. Find high-quality self-help materials to assist you. You can visit their Estate Planning Library to find books that can help you write the document. Do be cautious, however, as trust laws and taxation of trust assets is complicated. Establishing a trust without legal advice is possible but not recommended.

Remember to open the trust fund bank account. Take your signed agreement to a bank or financial institution to open your trust fund bank account. Open the account in the name of the trust. You will need the names and addresses of the trustees. Also, provide the bank with the names and contact information of anyone who will be authorized to access the trust fund account. File taxes for the trust. The trust is considered a separate legal entity, and a separate tax return must be filed. The trust will receive a deduction for any income distributed to beneficiaries, but the beneficiaries are responsible for paying the taxes on that income. You will need to complete Schedule B of Form

1041 for the trust, and the beneficiary must complete a Schedule K-1 form. Finally, the last step in setting up your trust is administering it following the trust's legal guidelines by keeping detailed records, including accounting records, so if there is ever a lawsuit or discrepancy, the paperwork is in order. At some point in your lifetime, or at the time of your death, you'll need to turn over these responsibilities to someone else.

THE IMPORTANCE OF BUYING LAND

It's amazing how many times people only dream to buy a single house instead of thinking bigger like buying land to place a house on. Think about it like this, a single house stays in your family a generation, or maybe two generations but land has the chance to stay in your family for years to come, and not hold just one house but potentially more. And with this land, you don't have to pay multiple property taxes but instead you'll just have to pay one land tax. Raw Land is a "Hands-Off" Investment. Have you had enough of dealing with tenants, toilets, bugs, mold, lawn care, leaking roofs, bursting pipes, broken furnaces, and the hundreds of other issues that come with owning buildings? Vacant land doesn't involve any of those things. Once you buy it, it sits there, it behaves itself, and nothing happens. I've said it before and I'll say it again, vacant land is one of the most overlooked and misunderstood real estate investments in the world. It's an unfortunate misconception because the truth is, vacant land is capable of producing some serious cash flow and it's one of the best investments on earth because of its hands-off nature and versatility. The simplicity and stability that comes with owning the right piece of land, purchased at the right price, can far outweigh the myriad of problems that come with any other type of real estate. If you've overlooked raw land as a viable investment opportunity in the past, you need to take a few minutes and get educated about what land is all about! With Vacant Land, You don't need to do anything to the Property. Forget construction! Forget renovations!

You don't need to be an expert, I say again, you don't need to be an expert or know anything about how to rehab a property yourself. In most cases, you really only need to know one thing: "Is the property suitable for building on it?" As long as someone else can build on the land if and/or when you want to, a huge part of the battle is already won. The land has an intrinsic ability to inspire us, give us serenity and help us to dream. Owning land can also be an excellent value. These tips reflect our wisdom gained from years of developing land for building a community or building generational wealth, observing changing markets, tax brackets, and real estate opportunities, and working with many different kinds of investors and stakeholders. Purchase land one to five years before you plan to build on it.

Pre-buying the land allows you to benefit from value appreciation, rather than paying that higher value later. Land is more fun to own than stocks.

The Roots of a Revolution

Just think of the board game Monopoly, pass go, buy lots and build on those lots to collect more income. There's a reason it's called "real" estate. When you own the land, you have the foundation to dream, plan and build your new home, homes, and legacy when the time is right. Plus, buying acreage gives you space, much more than crowded city lots. You can fit five city houses on a one-acre home-site.

There are lots of people who have never even considered buying land. You could find yourself asking "Is buying land a good investment?" Understandably so, people aren't always willing to play outside the box when it comes to their money. I'm not saying that buying land is the 'be all end all' of investing, but you should definitely be open to including it in your portfolio. You owe it to yourself to at least be educated about the different types of real estate investing. Most of you are familiar with the fancier and more glamorous real estate methods. House flipping, commercial real estate and home renovation shows take over TV channels. No one is talking about why land is a great investment. That presents you with an opportunity to grow, financially, physically, and mentally.

The Roots of a Revolution

Your family needs a set amount of land in order for your family to build generational wealth, something you can pass on to your kids and grand kids. Buildings can be replaced and demolished, whereas land is a valuable and finite resource, with only limited quantities available. My advice when looking to purchase a block of land is to look for something which has good building opportunity. If it is a sloping site you need to factor in additional excavation costs and foundation works and it would be best to choose a home design which suits a sloping block to reduce the foundation and excavation cost. Also, it is wise to carry out a Geotechnical Investigation to determine the ground classification, if rock, the cost for a rock breaker to do the excavation is on an hourly rate and could result in huge amounts more before you even commence construction of your home.

Alternatively, if the ground is too soft or there is a natural spring or ground water you will also be looking at additional costs for drill foundations down through this to stable ground. When looking at land, it is always good to get your builder to have a look, compare it to others for a square meter rate, start by assuming the block is flat and square, then subtract from there for things like slope, trees, irregular shapes etc. This will help you determine a fair market value.

The Roots of a Revolution

Before you purchase the block, be sure to research zoning regulations for both your property and the surrounding area. Councils have strict rules regarding what a block of land can be used for (residential, commercial, industrial). If the block next door could potentially develop into a warehouse or a five story apartment building it might not be the best option for your quiet retreat away from home. You'll also want to make sure there's no plans to build a highway or other infrastructure through your land or the nearby area. Depending on where your block of land is located, it could potentially be at risk to both fire and flooding.

These very real dangers can be avoided by consulting resources, which can help you determine flood zones as well as bushfires. State and local government councils will also have more information. Cross check occurrences over several years to get a clearer picture of how safe your new home will be from extreme acts of nature. New developments to take water saving measures with a target of reducing mains water usage by 40%. Many elect to use water tanks, however the proximity of your new home to creeks, rivers and dams can play a part in how attractive a block of land is as a potential home.

Yearly rainfall, temperature highs and lows, seasonal changes and even trends over the last 10 to 20 years are all factors to consider when looking purchasing the land. The climate affects many aspects of your life, including:

- How you insulate your home
- The types of plants and vegetables you can grow
- Potential for drought, frost and other extreme weather conditions
- The type of kit home appropriate for you block of land
- How much energy you might expect to use
- Health conditions like asthma that are affected by temperature

While you might not be able to have it all, knowing the climate of the local area can help you make a more informed decision. Statistically, vacant land owners are highly motivated to sell. Why you may ask? Because vacant landowners (by default) are always absentee owners, when a person doesn't live inside of (or even near) the property they're trying to sell, there is less of an "emotional connection" because it isn't their primary residence. In many cases, you'll find that these sellers are willing to sell their land for pennies on the dollar, simply because they don't live anywhere near it, it's not producing any income for them (because they don't know how to optimize their land correctly) and as a result, they are much more apathetic about it. Find these people, and you will find some incredible deals. Remember to look for a development property with "no time-frame to build." This is the best option if you want to pre-buy land with developer amenities and infrastructure. Land investors have very little competition to deal with. There is very little competition in the world of raw land investing. You see, most real estate investors have their minds stuck on things like houses, apartments, commercial property and the like, because that's what everyone else does. Buying land from a developer can save you money.

It's important to anticipate all future development costs and eliminate surprises. Is water supplied by the city, private water company or your own well? Will electric power be available at your property boundary? What about gas lines, sewage disposal and road maintenance? Will you want cable TV and Internet? When you buy from a land developer, the cost of infrastructure and modern amenities is part of the package up front, and because it is a shared community cost, it is less than developing the land yourself. Just like the soil quality and composition impacts both how your build your new home or homes and the potential for growing your own plants on your property. When it comes to building, soil composition can impact:

- Cost of building foundations
- Amount of earthworks required
- Stability and land retention

Contact a local and qualified engineer to have your soil tested before finalizing your build plans.

Orientation is one of the joys of designing your own home. By taking advantage of the 'north facing aspect, you can make use of available sunlight throughout the year while minimizing the impact of direct sunlight and the "greenhouse effect" to avoid overheating in the summer. The position of existing trees can play a significant role in your decision to purchase a block of land. While our natural fauna is beautiful and can add shade to the backyard, it can also pose a risk in extreme weather. Consider the impacts of falling branches or even whole trees on your home, particularly in storm affected areas. Removing trees is no easy task either. Fines for illegal removal of native trees can be excessive, so plan accordingly. Local councils can advise on tree removal and restriction.

However, when buying land you'll want to consider any existing easements, roads, driveways and the proximity of other structures both existing and potential (neighboring land).

Take for example, given a choice of two great views, make use of the one that isn't going to look into a neighbor's fence in a few years. Another important scenario you have to consider is what companies can connect your gas, electrical sewage and water? How much do they cost, and is there any competition? Rates can differ depending on where your new home is located, so take the time to source information about the companies that can provide your utilities. Contact them by phone for quotes, and ask locals in the area about their satisfaction with local utilities.

Most investors don't understand the superior benefits that come with land and this can definitely play to your advantage. When you buy vacant land the right way, it's easy to buy each property with your own cash and completely avoid dealing with banks and mortgage companies. When I got started as a land investor, I had $3,000 to my name and to this day, I have never had to borrow money from a bank, not ever. When you know where to look for great deals on land, it requires very little start-up capital to get your business up and running, no matter if its land, houses, a business or investing. When you learn how to research properties effectively, you can begin buying properties without even seeing it in person. In 2010, I bought and sold a parcel of land and grossed over $54,000. The entire process took me 6 months from start to finish and to this day, I've never actually seen this property with my own eyes. Everything was done virtually, using the tools that you and I have available for free online. The beauty of land is that it doesn't have to involve any structures. This means the inspection process is very simple, and if you're doing the right research, you can easily buy your properties without ever visiting them in person. Owning land near prime and/or up-and-coming growth areas means your property has a greater chance of increasing in value at a faster rate. Check the area for zoning, building codes, and other regulations to ensure the area will maintain its value for years to come.

Add Seller Financing to the mix and explode your Income Potential. The advantages of owning land can include: tax deductions, cash returns on the initial investment, and potential borrowing power. Many factors play a role in these benefits. The duration of ownership, property location and property value can enhance these benefits. Many people don't realize that land costs drops in the country, the further away from the city, the cheaper the acreage. Many people buy land because they want to build a home to their own specifications, or they want to build their own safe haven of generational wealth. They also want cleaner air and more wide open spaces. When you combine vacant land with the power of Seller Financing, it's a match made in heaven. It can open up the doors to finding many more buyers because most banks are very hesitant to lend money on vacant land. Due to the scarcity of "easy money" financing, a land investor can use this to their advantage by charging a higher-than-market interest rate and many people will gladly pay it. Seller financing is also a great way to create multiple streams of passive income that act like rental properties but come with virtually none of the typical headaches that rental properties are known for.

Land is very inexpensive to own as a long-term investment.

- Purchase high quality land for the best value.

- Natural beauty is universally attractive. The presence of trees, hills, picturesque views, and water access, often yield higher value over time.

- Be prepared to make a decision. Being a successful land buyer means being prepared to act. Do investigative homework. If you find the property perfect for your needs, don't wait. Don't let someone else beat you to it.

- Take advantage of developer discounts. Some developers offer discounts for purchasing more than 1 property at a time.

- Buy land with modern infrastructure. Modern conveniences add value to your property and increase your everyday enjoyment and comfort.

- Amenities enhance quality of life and increase resale value. Access to boating, fishing, swimming, and hunting add an extra appeal to property.

When you buy a piece of land for the right price, there are no mortgage payments to make, no utility bills to pay, the cost of property insurance is ostensible (if you have it at all) and property taxes are extremely cheap. If you want to park your cash somewhere and forget about it, vacant land could be exactly the investment vehicle you're looking for. Get all the information you need to make an informed and intelligent decision, because the reality of it is that buying land gives its owners peace of mind.

Think about it, land is a long-term, tangible asset that doesn't wear out, doesn't depreciate, and nothing can get broken, or destroyed, now stolen is another story just ask our ancestors, that's why you need to always make sure that your paperwork, will etc is up to date and accurate.. But if you place all of these benefits together with your ability to buy it for next-to-nothing, can you think of a better combination, probably not. Investing in land and buying land is not a well-understood concept. Most people don't know for sure how land buying works. And even fewer people understand how investing in land is a smart strategic move for diversifying your portfolio and becoming self-sufficient and building generational wealth. You don't want to be one of these people. Everyone knows the type, the kind of person that waits until they're to old to fix or even learn from their rerates.

It's not as if land can be manufacture and produced, they aren't making any more of It. Most people don't think of vacant land this way, but the reality is That land is an extremely valuable resource with limited quantities available. Especially when you purchase land in the path of growth, you will find yourself with a finite asset that a lot of other people want to get their hands on. Stocks, bonds, mutual funds, and 401Ks all make sense in certain scenarios, and so does land. If you go into this business adventure with the intent of holding the right property for the long-term, it can make a lot more sense and be a lot more profitable than any other retirement vehicle out there.

Now obviously, I wouldn't recommend pulling the trigger on anything like this unless you're ready to take it seriously and treat it like a business or at least as a vessel to help your family become more self-suffocate. If you think you've got what it takes and you're ready to dive in. Planning is the most important secret to acquiring the property of your dreams. Having your down payment in hand allows you to make a decision the same day, ahead of competitive buyers who may be considering the same property. Being a successful land buyer means being prepared to act. Do investigative homework prior to the visit and be prepared to use that knowledge to maximize your financial leverage. And if you find the perfect property for your needs on your first visit, don't wait. Don't let someone else beat you to the bargaining table.

BUILDING GENERATIONAL WEALTH

The imperceptible markers of generational wealth and self-sufficiency are manifold, from the promise of a good education to the security of homeownership. Wealth begets further wealth, but not always through inheritance of assets. Much of the transmission of wealth to the next generation goes through these earlier life processes, such as supporting children's education, supporting their ability to purchase a home, or to get married. Self-sufficiency is the quality of feeling secure and content with oneself, a deep-rooted sense of inner completeness and stability. All of these, building a business or your own business, education, homeownership, marriage, in turn help you accumulate wealth. On a superficial level, it's similar to secure self-esteem; it's an estimation of oneself as a worthy and decent person. But it goes deeper than secure self-esteem, in that it's not just a cognitive but also an affective state, that is, it's a feeling of fundamental wholeness and well-being. Rather than thinking in terms of high or low, as with self-esteem, it seems more appropriate to use the terms weak and strong for self-sufficiency. People with strong self-sufficiency aren't too concerned with other people's opinions of them.

Slights don't affect them so much, because they have a deep-rooted sense of their own worth. Conversely, praise and blame don't affect them too much either, so that they never become too carried away with their own good fortune or self-importance. By definition, generational wealth represents assets passed down from one generation to the next. If you can leave behind a notable inheritance to your descendants, that constitutes generational wealth. These assets can include real estate, stock market investments, a business, or anything else which contains monetary value. People who inherit generational wealth have a significantly existential financial advantage over those who do not. They will more likely have the ability to avoid student loans as well as other types of costly debt. Instead, their inheritance could go towards income-generating investments, assets which appreciate in value, or even towards purchasing their first home.

Growing up without an inheritance, will make you and your family feel the financial, physical and emotional set-backs, but the burden of the set-backs doesn't have to be a burden for long. By educating you, your family and especially your children on financial discipline, on positive and structured financial habits and goals. You see it's easy to go out and purchase brand new items, houses, cars, etc as soon as they hit the market, but the question you must first ask yourself is, do you really need what you are about to purchase? And would this purchase bring value in your life? The fact stands that there's always going to be a new item, new home, and new car, just because we have to money to purchase the item doesn't mean that we have enough money to support and/or keep the item of purchase. Each purchase should bring more than admiration within our lives, each purchase and especially each big purchase should bring growth and sufficiency to you and your family's life.

The same applies to negative or positive life events: people with strong self-sufficiency are less likely to be destabilized by them. This doesn't mean that they're inhuman monsters who don't feel any emotions, just that they have a strong internal centre of gravity and you need a balance way of thinking in order to begin building generational wealth, likely to be stoical and theoretical about negative events and to bounce back quickly. Their inner sense of well-being and completeness means that they're more resilient to the vicissitudes of life, and your mental placement shows in each one of your big purchases. Generational wealth and self-sufficiency is associated with certain traits. Self-sufficient people have a strong internal locus of control, discipline and determination. That is, they have the ability and the desire to determine their own course, to make their own decisions, rather than having their life choices made by others. They trust in their own instincts and abilities, and are prepared to go their own way, even if it means going against the expectations of others, and so facing incomprehension and ridicule. However, it's not easy to maintain Self-sufficiency or generational wealth across several generations without financial discipline. In fact, research shows approximately 70% of families lose their capital in the second generation while 90% lose it in the third. Not great odds for building sustainable wealth over several generations. To generate wealth that you can pass on, you need to acquire assets and/or save money you won't need to spend in your retirement. You then pass down the money and/or assets to children or other younger relatives. While the concept is simple, unless you had wealth passed down to you, accumulating extra assets can be slow. Fortunately, it's entirely possible if you are strategic with your finances. These four strategies are the most accessible paths toward building generational wealth. Try Investing in stocks, CD's accounts, and buying land. Stocks and CD's are arguably one of the best ways to build long-term wealth over time. Some people recommend starting by investing in index funds that carry low costs. An index fund is a type of mutual fund or exchange-traded fund (ETF) meant to match the components of a market index. However, in terms of generational wealth, your initial goal focuses on capital appreciation as you set aside more money and your investments grow in value. As you age and wish to take less risk, you transition toward a capital preservation strategy. This is a similar strategy baked into the best target date funds, which automatically transition the fund's holdings over time as you near your target retirement date.

1. Create Multiple Sources of Income

Start with a Full-Time Job, get to work! A full-time job provides you with stable income that you can funnel into saving and investing. Plus, hopefully it provides benefits like a 401K and Health Savings Account, which are great investment tools. But, and there is a BUT, your full-time job isn't enough to help you create long-term, long-lasting, generational wealth. In order to do this, you have to have multiple sources of sticking income. Income is like snow, if it begins to snow but doesn't stick, most likely the snow will be gone by the next day. Your income works the same way, if you're making a steady income but if half or over half of your income is going right back out of the door into your day to day life, that means that your income isn't sticking.

The Roots of a Revolution

If you don't remember anything else, remember that your family, time, effort and energy are true wealth. Not money, materialistic precession, how many friends or followers you have, not being obsessed about having nice things, etc. in order to build a great empire and legacy, it's important that first knowing yourself and what is true value and second, what brings peace of mind and meaning to your life. Generational wealth isn't grown over night, but it can all be spent in one night. Our focus in helping our finances stick is in centering and structuring our lives. So how do you create multiple sources of income and peace of mind at the same time?

There are a few ways of doing this but the most effective ways in my opinion, are to consider a side-hustle that will actually be more beneficial towards your building and not beneficial towards your downfall. Everyone would like to have a little extra money coming in, especially if it comes by way of doing something you love to do, the question is when it comes to really doing something you love, what comes to mind for you?

Maybe it's writing book, or providing a service like doing hair or cutting grass, or maybe it's starting up businesses one by one with 20 investors/co business owners, and help each other build and stabilize each other's dreams and visions. Either way these are a couple of common examples of fruitful side-hustles but there are a lot of ways you can work a little more to make more. Productive side-hustles can have a big impact on your income in the long run if you leverage your money and time wisely. But the extent to which family money helps future generations retain and build on their wealth, or acquire financial literacy, is less marked than you might imagine. You want to invest this money back into your business or side-hustle to expand its possibilities for the future. Or maybe you want to invest this money into maxing out your retirement account. This cash isn't just extra spending power. If you think of it that way, you will lose it. You should consistently utilize the cash from your side-hustle as an important part of your greater financial plan and invest it in your goals. If you do this, the additional funds you'll make can help you build wealth and the impact will be monumental for future generations. But do you need to work more to make more?

Pay attention to how affective your side-hustle and/or business and on the effects it is having on your long-term goals, but also on your current family and happiness. Weigh out all of the pros and cons. Is your side-hustle or business really benefiting you and your family? If the answer is

"NO," it is time to think critically about how you can better invest your time and effort and energy. If nothing comes to mind when you think about your business or side-hustle, or if you are looking for a hustle don't be so quick to think of a side-job, a side job is to drain your time with not very much reward, but a promising side hustle if structured correctly can shot you into a new tax bracket that won't take up too much of your time. Consider this, Investing into a CD, investing in stock, investing in real-estate, investing period. Investing is a relatively low-commitment side-hustle that doesn't require a large amount of effort to be successful. When most people think of investing as a job, they think of day-trading. Practices like this is where people make risky choices in the stock market that often don't work out. That's not what we are talking about here.

Remember the founding investing principle of Rule; #1: Don't lose money! Investors focus on long-term investments that won't lose money. This smart type of investing allows you cash flow now and a big return on your money in the long-term future. Once you learn the basics of investing, you will be able to buy the right kind of companies, services, and/or items and provide income for you and your family with very little effort. We call this income from investing passive income. Passive income is crucial in building generational wealth.

The Roots of a Revolution

Passive income is money you don't have to work for in the traditional sense. You don't have to go into an office or complete certain tasks to earn it. This is the stream of income that some of the wealthiest individuals rely on, using the consumers to make money for them. Investing is the best generator of passive income and getting into a more self-suffocate tax bracket. With a little bit of work on the front end, you can sit back and watch your money generate more money all on its own. It's a little bit like planting a seed in the ground. You do the work to plant the seed and then watch it grow, and it can grow in an exponential way. Like most things in life, when learning how to invest, the more you put into it, the better you will be. Creating wealth that will last from generation to generation is not a task for the lazy.

It is important to continue to learn new things both in investing and in general. When you get comfortable, you stop paying attention to how your decisions are affecting your well-being and the well-being of your family. So pay attention, and keep learning. Staying up to date will not only impact your success as a business entrepreneur but also an investor but also your happiness in other areas of your life. Now that you have earned some extra money, both actively and passively, you are on your way towards building generational wealth.

But just a quick reminder, trying to be anyone and everyone's financial saver will not only damage your relationship and/or marriage, but your home financial foundation as well. It's ok to do for family and/or friends but you must understand that your household stability should always come first. How do you hold onto it? No amount of money will keep a fool rich or a foolish giver wealthy. So spend it wisely. Because there's one thing to say that you were never taught something, and there's another thing to not aim to educate yourself.

There are a few common money traps people fall into when it comes to spending money.
You don't want to be one of them.

1. You don't have enough emergency funds saved to rely on when things go wrong
2. You don't have enough money invested in the stock market, which is the single best option to get a return on your investment.
3. You buy things you don't really need, like a flashy new car, a bigger house, a grand vacation.
4. Overly funding family and friends
5. Investing in opportunities that have no financial structure or stability.
6. The best way to lose money is telling people you have it.

Here is how to avoid these traps:

- Pay yourself first! Put the first 10% of your paycheck or earnings into savings.
- Invest in a CD's, 3,000 or at least a 1,000 in one year, the third year, the fifth year, the seventh year, and the tenth year with rates that's 2.3 or above.
- Think long term! Do your best to avoid the material things that are here today and passé tomorrow. Buying the flashy new car this year, or simply keeping up with the Jones is going to cost you way more than buying the same model a year or two later. Buy when you need to and invest the rest.

Whether you have fallen into one or all of these traps, you are never too far gone to make a change. The sooner you start to shift your mindset and learn to spend wisely, the better off you and your family will be.

Here are some of the commonly held misconceptions about the beneficiaries of generational wealth.

1. THEIR WEALTH LASTS MANY GENERATIONS

We don't have to look further than to see how wealth can trickle down and set up future generations for success. But generational wealth is actually harder to maintain than America's richest families might lead you to believe: About 70% of wealthy families lose their wealth by the second generation, and 90% do by the following generation. One reason that happens is the follow generation may not be equipped or has properly learned how to manage the money they inherit. But it's also that family wealth can be diluted as it is divided amongst partners, siblings, and children, especially if each has a different stance on how to invest or manage the family finances. Not unlike businesses, families need to come up with a "mission statement" to establish financial values and goals, in an effort to preserve wealth and stability across future generations. You might think parents with money share their financial know-how with their offspring. But that's not necessarily the case. Some parents don't want their kids to feel like they have a huge landing pad or that they may not need to work. A lot of times, they don't talk to them about money at all. That can mean parents not only don't disclose how much their kids stand to inherit but also don't necessarily offer guidance on how they should spend and invest their money. What's surprising is, I find that a lot of them get to their thirties, forties, maybe even fifties and still don't really know anything about money.

Sometimes, even financial advisers make assumptions about people who have money, presuming, for example, that they are well-versed in investing. In truth, the folks who inherit tens of millions of dollars may know less about money, and especially investing, than someone who saved a million dollars.

2. THEY KNOW WHAT TO DO WITH THEIR MONEY

Some wealthy folks don't turn to financial professionals until they inherit wealth and have to deal with large sums of money. Advisers may throw around acronyms or sophisticated terms that they don't quite understand. Once these assumptions are made, it's hard for them to speak up and say, "I have no idea what you're talking about," I have clients who've inherited a lot of money but may not even know [the difference] between a stock and bond, a CD and a Trust, or know the importance of buying land over buying a house. Working in the psychology field brings you more closely towards having a more understanding of a clear financial space. reading and learning to aim towards having your home and income in a more financial space can also mean you're moving in a better direction towards having a total understanding of financial literacy. Even people who work at hedge funds or in private equity, who are considered money managers, in so many words, don't trust a person to be over your money and livelihood just because they have a title. Check into people backgrounds; monitor their reviews because they may not be particularly well-versed in personal investing. Most people that are well-off, they're not necessarily thinking about how to pay for college or give their children money down the road. The weight of a hefty inheritance can also be a source of stress for the beneficiaries of generational wealth, even more so if they aren't financially knowledgeable.

Depending on how their or your wealth were accumulated or inherited, it can actually be very complicated and cause a lot of financial stress. Inherited individual retirement accounts require distributions and are taxed as regular income. Trusts accounts may have very stringent restrictions on what the money can be used for, and if the money is not managed properly, there can be significant emotional and financial consequences. Most people's financial habits are informed by those of their parents or people of their surroundings. It's no different for the children of wealthy parents or people that grew up without a lot. People, who build their own wealth from basically nothing or from nothing, are usually more frugal; often they feel lucky to have money they never expected to have and spend accordingly. Future generations born into wealth may spend more freely, but chances are hopefully, they'll take notes from how their parents approached money.

Once you have your family and your own spending habits under control, it is time to start investing the funds you have saved up or accumulated. Don't wait for a financial advisor or a fund manager to tell you to put your money in the stock market, or a CD or invest it in something that will inline your pockets and bank account more than just drain it. You have the knowhow, and you can start right now. Why start now? The first question you must ask yourself is how long it will take to double your money given a fixed interest rate. Take for example, if you want your money to double in three years, you can figure out the average annual rate of return you will need to get on your money each year by dividing 72 by 3 and surprise the answer will always end up being 24. So you are looking for an investment that can give you a 24% annual return on every investment you make.

Still kind of confused? Ok look at it this way, Say you can expect an annual interest rate of 12%. How long will it take you to double your money?
Divide 72 by 12 and you'll get 6.
So, it will take you about 6 years to double your money with a 12% annual rate of return on your

investment. The sooner you invest in a company with a high annual rate of return, the sooner you can double your money. Time is the friend of a wonderful business investment and the enemy of a lousy business investment. When building your kingdom and generational wealth, it's always a good idea to keep track of how much money is coming in and how much money is going out. Investing now in your personal business or in an investment, is the quickest and easiest way to build wealth over time. If you choose to invest in businesses with high compounding annual rates of return, your money grows for you, without you having to actually do anything! This brings us back to passive income.

There are several types of investments to choose from. But not all investments can help you generate passive income. If you start up and begin owning a wonderful business or businesses, you are going to have great chance at a compounding machine and that compounding machine will continue to generate wealth for you. If you look at the wealthiest not the richest but the wealthiest people in the world, you can attribute a great deal of their wealth to the businesses they own. And you too can be an owner of businesses by believing and investing in yourself, because working everyday for someone else is never going to get you there.

Think about investing, if a company is compounding money at a rate of 30% per year. If you invested in that company ten years ago, your equity would have doubled every 2.4 years for the past 10 years. Like for example, investing in Apple stocks, pay attention to supply and demand, consistent products are always great investment vessels. There is nothing else on the planet that compounds money as quickly or greatly as that. This is the most perfect way to generate passive income.

Invest in your child or children's education, and remember that your children learn from you just as much as they learn from schools, so guide them towards their greatness. If you want your children to be effective and avid readers, they must see you being an effective and fervent reader. The term "I don't like to read or I don't have time to read", should never be in your vocabulary. If you want your children to be able to provide for themselves and their children, even better than you did for them, invest in your children's education, skills, talents etc. Send them to college. Provide them with all of the education and resources they need to be successful on their own, but make sure that they're pulling their own weight. There's a difference in helping your children and hindering your children. Overly doing for your children and not allowing your child to fail and learn from their failures and decisions is hindering them from them from their greatness. At the very least, this background will provide them with the work ethic and understanding they need to successfully manage the money they earn or inherit. If worst comes to worst, it will also provide them with the resources they need to make it on their own if their money dries up for any number of reasons. As parents, it's our job to make sure our children are taken care of. And while that means investing in their education and providing for them financially, it's so much more than that. We want to be able to train them up in the way they should go so that they won't stray from it when they grow up. This couldn't be truer when it comes to teaching them about productive money and unproductive habits. You can leave your kids with a nest egg, sure, but the tools you provide them with are crucial in ensuring they will be able to sustain and grow that wealth for generations to come.

Working with an attorney to create a will on its own will not create wealth but it can help your loved ones manage and preserve the wealth you've accumulated. Essentially a will is a legal document that expresses how a person's assets should be dispersed. It is important to note however that beneficiaries listed on your accounts will normally supersede a will. Having a will can give your family specific instructions for what to do with your assets and who will receive them, taking the guesswork out of the process. Building generational wealth isn't something that is going to happen overnight. However, with small, consistent steps over time, the moves you make today can help propel generations for decades to come.

If you truly want to create generational wealth for your family, it is essential that you pass down more than just materialistic passions, money from negative resources, unhealthy sex habits, and arrogance to your heirs. You must also teach them all of the knowledge and lessons you have accumulated over the years or if you were blessed the same lessons that allowed you to become wealthy in the first place. What are the skills you utilized to create wealth? Hard work? Perseverance? Resourcefulness? Discipline? Teamwork? Building a strong supportive circle around you? Whatever it was you can teach your kids some of these skills by example and some by sitting down with them and having a conversation. Anything less and your wealth may not last more than a single generation. Make sure that you are spending quality time with your children and teaching them life gems. How do you expect your children to know how to preserve money, be accountable, be reasonable, be responsible, and walk with integrity if you don't teach them? Most importantly, you have to teach them the value of these things. Then, you can teach them the skills to save, invest, and manage these things wisely, especially their integrity. The best way to pass on these lessons is to spend quality time with your children. Spending time when you can have a conversation about all the different ways you can invest, and how to handle money conservatively so they or their children don't squander what they have been given.

Show them what type of life good financial planning can provide. Take the time to talk with them about how you got here and the type of person you need to not only present but be when no one is watching. And let us remember, there are more important things than money, attention and material precisions. The simple act of sitting down with your family to discuss these topics in and of itself can provide priceless connection. But sometimes no matter how much effort we place in our children, sometimes our children and/or grand-children may still stray from what has be taught. When it comes down to the control you will have over your family's wealth and well-being after you're gone, an estate plan and will are essential. With these tools you can set up your kids, grandkids, and future generations with the tools they need to handle the wealth you built. That's why financial education and teaching kids the value of money can go a long way; make sure this is a priority when building your generational wealth plan.

FINAL THOUGHT

There's a saying floating around deep within everyone subconscious that says, "Cooler heads will always prevail and make change, while tempered heads will always resort to anger and will always be easily distracted." No matter the race, we all bring something unique and beautiful to the world but some people either do not care about the power of unity and unified growth or they're just consumed by their hatred and/or greed. Instead of being divided and trying to divide each other, we must aim to understand and respect each other's diversity and what we all bring to the world as a whole. We are all talented in something; we must drive to be successful in our talents in-order to provide productivity to our communities.

It doesn't matter your talent or craft, if you are looking to be the best you cannot let limitations hinder you. If you want to be great in your own right you must remember to stay in that lane, you don't have time for anything else outside of that lane. Stop letting obstacles cripple you or define your abilities. In order to be successful you must create a kill list in life, instead of concerning yourself with the number one person while you're in twenty-fifth place is a pointless concern. Instead of you bettering yourself for twenty-four place, twenty-third place and so on, you set your shots to high before you are even ready. Success is built on determination, drive, accountability, and your mental strength. We as a culture need to get out of survival-mode in-order to conquer all of life's obstacles and stop letting them obstacles define and cripple us and our families, mentally, emotionally, physically and spiritually. Oppression is here to crush our spirits, but oppression can't crush your work ethic. Not if you use the world as your mental library, and learn from the obstacle instead of repeating the obstacle and allowing obstacle to define you. Instead of always asking what people can do for you and add to your life, ask yourself what you can do for others and add to the people in your circle life. Be one of those type of people who make other people life better by just being in it and not make people resentful for you being in their life.

In our culture, each and every day is a fight to stay above water. We must arm ourselves with mental substance, emotional substance, and motivational stimulating conversations with substance. Remember our time is limited, so never waste a moment living someone else's life, and just live yours. Think about it like this, if you improve yourself and your life by 1% everyday, within a year you will have improved your life by 365%, think about it.

They're five rules of wealth and five rules of peace of mind.

6 rules of wealth
1. Save at least 10% of your income.
2. Invest your money to multiply it.
3. Don't fall for any get rich quick scams or a bunch of (woe is me) down on my luck stories.
4. Keep learning new fruitful things with substance daily.
5. Diversify your portfolio.
6. If you are a giver know your limits because the takers don't have any limits.

6 rules of peace of mind
1. Hold yourself accountable for your actions.
2. Do not let the behavior of others destroy who you are as a person nor your inner peace.
3. Realize and know your worth and have self-love'
4. Being true to who you are as a person, loving self and others unconditionally.
5. Having goals and working toward those goals to achieve them.
6. Appreciate the simple things in your life.

True peace is the result of restraining your mind to process life as it is, rather than as you think it should be.

Question your lifestyle and see if it's truly being beneficiary to your life. How are you going to have 20 friends to go out drinking and partying with, but not have 1 single friend to open up a business or two with? If you're circle actions isn't matching up with your actions for change than you need to change the people in your circle. The only person that can hold you and your family back from being successful and prospering is you and your family and who you all decide to surround yourselves with.

When you don't have healthy boundaries, you'll probably;

1. Wait for people to figure out what you needed.
2. Allow people to borrow money that you couldn't afford to loan.
3. Easily say "yes" to things you didn't have time to do.
4. You'll spend money without considering your family and/or finances.
5. You'll allow people to borrow items and not have enough respect for you to return them.
6. You'll offer to help in cases where you did not have the capacity to.

7. Do what people wanted of you without considering you or your family's needs.
8. Tell people what was best for them and you haven't even figured out what's best for you yet.
9. You'll make yourself available to people when you didn't have the time.
10. You are a easy quitter, meaning you give up on everything that present you with a challenge, Marriage, relationships, jobs, family, etc.
11. You'll often feel resentful towards people for asking you to help them and then later get mad at yourself for doing it.

Our diet is the most important thing in this world. I'm not just talking about diet as in eating but diet as in an eating diet, sleeping diet, mental diet, negativity diet, fake friend's diet, toxic relationship/marriage diet, and so on. Some people make the excuse of being in a dark place, that's why they were entertaining foolishness. It's not darkness that you were in; it was more of a depression-state of settling. We need to stop associating darkness with scariness, evil and bad. Like when you close your eyes to kiss, dream, sleep, relax or meditate we go into the darkness. The dark night sky allows us to see the moon and the stars shining. Most of the universe is in constant darkness. When we plant a seed in the ground or the new life a mother carries, we place them into darkness to grow. Darkness is the breeding ground for creation and life. Embrace the light and the kindness of the darkness equally as one cannot exist without the other. Within the darkness, lessons can be learned and true growth can be acquired.

The key lies in paying attention to the seeds. You see, you can't sell dreams to someone who has walked through nightmares, and as a culture for 400 years we've been walking through nightmares. We have to realize that we can't change the mind of the people that are benefiting off of the nightmares of our oppression, but we can help change the minds of the oppress. We have been stereotyped as lazy every since we've stopped working for free, we've been stereotyped as criminals every since they found out how to legally turn us into prison profits. As a people we've been oppressed for so long we have begun to oppress ourselves. Our unity as a culture should make us feel safe, loved, happy, unified, and supported, not tense, anxious, and scared. As a culture we must realize that self – control is strength and calmness is mastery. Our culture as a whole have to get to a point where our mood doesn't shift based on the insignificant actions of someone else. We must stop allowing others to control the direction of our life. Don't allow your emotions to overpower your intelligence.

Remember nothings impossible, but to someone that knows their worth & roots and realize that they are destined for greatness, impossible is nothing. Stop being afraid of obstacles, obstacles are there to challenge us and shape us to be ready when it's time to fulfill our purpose in life. the question you must ask yourself is do you want to build your own empire and validate yourself or do you want you and your family to continue being treated like presences within someone else empire or kingdom continuously looking for validation from others? No matter what your choice is, whether to conquer your obstacles or rather continue to be oppressed by them the answer will be the same; deliver no excuses, just results!

SOUTH KOREA

BLACK OWNED BUSINESSES

Beauty & Health

Honey Beauty Supply
Owner: Jessica Fry
Address: 222 Beongil Building 106,
Paengseong-eup Anjeongri, Pyeongtaek, Gyeonggi-do 17982
Phone number: 031-655-5307
Social Media:
https://www.facebook.com/HoneyHairKorea/

Entertainment

DJ
Owner: DJ Juise
Address: Camp Humphrey's
Social Media: IG: djjuise
Twitter: Djjuise813 Snap Chat: datboijuise
Email: djjuise@gmail.com

DJ
Owner: Tee Blaze

Phone number: 01027795657
Social Media: @djteeblaze
Email: djteeblaze@gmail.com

Food & Drinks

Island Bites Restaurant Bar Coffee

Owner:King
Address: 319-5 Sinjang-dong, Pyeongtaek-si,
Gyeonggi-do
Phone Number: 031-666-1336

JJ's American Diner

Owner: Jessica Fry
Address: 113-88 Anjeongri, Pyeongtaek, Gyeonggi-
do 17983
Phone number: 031-8094-1337
Social Media:
https://www.facebook.com/jjsdinerkorea/

JJ's Jazz and Funk Lounge

Owner: Jessica Fry
Address: 9
3-4 Anjeogsunhwan-ro 222beon-gil,
Paengseong-eup Pyeongtaek-si, Gyeonggi-do
Pyeongtaek 17982
Phone number: 031-658-9304

Social Media: https://www.facebook.com/JJs-Jazz-and-Funk-Lounge

Catering

African dish in Korea

Owner: Sophie

Phone number: 01046380247

Helpful Resources

Bolld Connect International

Address: 233 TianHeBei Rd. 5F Block A18-3
TianHe District, Guangzhou 510000
Social Media:
WeChat: Bolld Connect International
Linkedin: Bolld Connect International
Instagram: @Bolldconnect
Facebook: Bolld Connect International
What you offer: Translation, Subtitles,Localization,
International Trademark Assistance, Education
Consulting, Business Licensing Assistance

Home Goods

Wasteupso- The Zero Waste Shop

Owner: Kychele Boone

Phone number: +82 010-2733-6631
Address: Seoulsi Seochogu Bangbaero 189 4th
floor
Social Media:
Instagram: @wasteupso_thezerowasteshop
Facehook:Wasteupso
What the offer: zero waste products, home goods
and foods.

Marketing

East Meets west Korea
-Phone number: 01089767833

JR Consulting
Phone number: 01083079015
Address: Juan Dong 882-1, incheon, South Korea
Social Media: https://jobsandresume.com
Facebook: Jobs and resumes
Instagram: jobsandresumes.com
What we offer:
1. Resume writing and Consultation
2. Applicant Tracking System (ATS) resume scan
3. Linkedin Optimization
4. ATS friendly resume templates

Shops

The Roots of a Revolution

Paparazzi

Owner: Fidiqua Morant
Address: Camp Casey, S. Korea
Phone number: 010-3917-7189
Social Media: Boots 2 Bling VIP Fam
www.PaparazziAccessoriess.com/ConsultantID

Songtan Mugs

Owner: Jason V. Holmes
Address: Osan Sed
Phone number: 010-2590-9281
Social Media: @Songtanmugs